P9-DNB-656

ALSO BY ROBERTA ISRAELOFF

Coming to Terms

In Confidence

Why Parents Disagree and What You Can Do About It (with Ron Taffel)

Lost and Found

A Woman Revisits Eighth Grade

ROBERTA ISRAELOFF

SIMON & SCHUSTER

SIMON & SCHUSTER
Rockefeller Center
1230 Avenue of the Americas
New York, NY 10020

Designed by Irving Perkins Associates

Manufactured in the United States of America

1 3 5 7 9 10 8 6 4 2

Library of Congress Cataloging-in-Publication Data
Israeloff, Roberta, date.
Lost and found : a woman revisits eighth grade / Roberta Israeloff
p. cm.
1. Israeloff, Roberta, date—Childhood and youth. 2. Teenage
girls—United States—Psychology. 3. Junior high school
students—United States. 4. Self-perception in adolescence—
United States. 5. Eighth grade (Education) I. Title.
HQ798.I785 1996
305.23'5—dc20 96-12318 CIP
ISBN 0-684-80081-0

This story is based upon the author's experiences in the eighth grade. The names of all the students and teachers have been changed.

ACKNOWLEDGMENTS

I'd like to thank Lorene Vorbach Bossong, Tonia Hysko, Carole Green, Eileen Morrone, Joan Reminick, Celeste Wenzel, and Elizabeth Wix for being endlessly encouraging and patient with me and this book since its inception; Laurel Brett for generously sharing her remembrances and insights; Wallace Kaufman for answering (and saving) my first and every subsequent letter; Denise Roy and Marjorie Shain Horvitz for their cheerful expertise in overseeing and editing the manuscript; Carol Rubin for setting certain key events in motion; Pam Abrams, Alice Alexiou, Diane Cole, Vicki Lens, Dena Salmon, and Elly Silberman for conversation that never quits; Ron Taffel for believing and for always understanding.

I'm especially indebted to Becky Saletan for her vision, enthusiasm, inspired editorial suggestions, and unflagging faith in this book.

To Lynn Seligman, a special thank-you yet again for guidance, hand-holding, and support every step of the circuitous and rewarding way.

Finally, heartfelt thanks to Anne Thompson; to Ellen Ostrow for all the arm-in-arm miles we've logged during thirty-plus years of friendship, which grows blessedly richer as we grow older; to Ben and Jake for reminding me how it feels to be a kid; and to David for more than I could possibly say.

Finally, for Jacob

Adolescence thus seems a watershed
in female development, a time when
girls are in danger of drowning or
disappearing.

—Carol Gilligan,
Making Connections

To be careless, dauntless, to create havoc—that
was the lost hope of girls.

—Alice Munro,
"Open Secrets"

PROLOGUE

Eight A.M. My older son, a sixth grader, shoulders his backpack and leaves to walk to school. His younger brother, six years old, left half an hour ago. I close the door behind me and lock it twice. On my way to the kitchen I stop, listening to the sighs and creaks of a settling house. "I'm alone," I make myself say out loud. "No one else is here. Just me."

For the first time in twelve years, I've achieved parity, spending roughly as many of my waking hours in my own company as I do in my children's.

In the kitchen, I wipe the counter, wash their breakfast dishes, dry them and put them immediately away, as if I'm erasing their very traces. Climbing the stairs to my study, I ponder formulas like a mathematician seeking some encoded message. If I divide the eighteen years that I assume my children will live with me into thirds, then Ben is entering his last lap; Jake, his second. They stand at the respective cusps of adolescence and latency, each taking a significant step out of the house. Early-phase mothering, during which I knew every thought as it flickered behind their eyes, each half inch of their bodies, what they ate and excreted, is long over. Though not yet a physical reality, my childbearing days are history. I'm forty-two: half my life over, half to go, statistically speaking.

"So many women our age are getting cats or dogs, have you noticed?" mused a friend at lunch the other day.

"Oh, God," I said, a trifle too loud, the disgust in my voice startling both of us. "Not me." The care of living creatures on an intimate, day-to-day basis is something I am in the midst of bidding good-bye. The thought of signing on for more made me shudder.

But what's next? I have the shank of the day entirely at my disposal. I'm free to take a walk before getting down to work, to call a friend for lunch, to browse in the library. Free from having to fit all my work and household chores and personal responsibilities into the erose spaces my children's schedules carve out for me. Now, when my dentist asks, "When can you come in?" I don't have to say, "Between ten forty-five and eleven-thirty on Tuesdays or Thursdays"—the thin sliver of time between dropping one child off and picking up another. Now I can say, with undisguised incredulity, "Anytime."

At the threshold of my older son's room, I sigh. He lives among indescribable clutter. I close his door, and his brother's, so I won't see their clothes, their toys, their schoolbooks, when I pace the hallway. My freedom, I realize, stretches beyond today or next week; it extends for the rest of my life. The giant Ferris wheel of motherhood, which swept me off my feet twelve years ago, has deposited me back on land, and I feel both the disorientation and the apprehension I always feel when a ride is over, when it's time to smooth my hair back into place, look around, and find my companions. What's next? Theoretically I can do anything—become a lawyer, a psychologist, a doctor. Reactivate my teaching license. Open a computer software store. Learn ancient Greek and read Sophocles.

I pause at the door to my study. This is a true crossroads, not simply empty-nest syndrome. If anything, I feel the opposite of bereft. Something—or, more accurately, someone—is rising up inside me; an internal voice I haven't heard in years has returned after a long banishment. Whose voice? Why now?

I switch on my computer. With electronic beeps and grunts as familiar and comforting as the sounds of the house, it rouses itself into binary awareness. Almost instantaneously it's at attention, cursor dumbly winking at me, ready for my command.

But this morning I'm distracted. To the side of my computer rests a pile of dime-store diaries. For years I'd lost track of them, knowing they existed without knowing where. I didn't set out to find them but rather stumbled upon them recently, as I looked for something else, in a dusty box in a corner of my parents' basement. The first one, a palm-sized volume with a red vinyl cover and a miniature bronze key and clasp, is dated January 1, 1964—exactly thirty years ago. I was twelve, the same age as Ben.

I remember where I purchased it—in the Woolworth's

on Bell Boulevard in Bayside, Queens, which sported wooden floors and overhead fans—but not why. I remember the thrill of flipping through the pages, each stamped with the date—but not in which room I wrote, or at what time of day.

When I try to summon these memories, I see my mother sitting at her desk in the living room, holding her green enamel fountain pen, a gift from my father, her arm sweeping across the page in beautiful looping script. She paid bills, wrote notes to friends, answered letters from a man for whom she used to work before she had children. The ink, a rich turquoise, took time to dry; sometimes she'd hold the check or letter between two fingers and gently wave or blow on it. She was apart from us, seated at her desk, as if she had drawn a thick drape around herself. I never interrupted her, just watched her hand move across the paper. She seemed infinitely far away.

Had I been drawn to the solitude that seemed to descend on a writer? Or was it the lock on the diary itself that attracted me, the tiny island of privacy it granted me within the room I shared with my younger sister? Or was I simply fascinated with the seeming permanence of the written word?

I flip through the thin pages, now brittle with age, upon which I wrote so forcefully that the words are palpable, like Braille. Entire entries are devoted to the recounting of baseball games, test scores, analyses of homework assignments, plans for the future.

JANUARY 27:

Dear Dee, Dahling, I've made up my mind. . . . If all goes well, God permitting, here's my future: I'm gonna go to college and go out in the peace corp or someplace in the U.S. helping poorer people and develop crazy ideas. At about 26, I'll marry and have kids at about 28. Middle age motherhood for me!! It's better than getting married early! Hope this works out!!

Who *wrote* that? I think to myself, embarrassment and indignation rising in equal measure. Certainly not me. Even the handwriting looks like an impostor's. I was never the type to write "Dahling" or sprinkle exclamation points so liberally, I insist, eager to disown the volume, to fling it aside.

Yet I cannot. It *is* mine, a testament in black and white to my innermost thoughts and reflections. Though at moments it is ditsy and girlish, its overriding tone is forceful and confident, even when I'm writing about marriage and childbirth. It's riddled with swagger, peppered with curses—in short, undeniably masculine.

FEBRUARY 9:

We're probably buying the house!!! I've changed from fear to wanting. Mom and Dad seem so eager, I couldn't disappoint them. I hope like hell I can finish school here but if not, well OK. So excited! Think I'll major in physics in college. Kids there must be nice. I'm sure everything will work out just fine.

This is how I greeted the news that my parents had decided, in the winter of 1964, to move from an apartment in Queens to a house in the suburbs. I'd just begun to feel comfortable in seventh grade, with a coterie of friends, good teachers, and even a boy who liked me. The news that we'd be moving must have hit me with seismic force.

Yet optimism suffuses the diary entry—my father's optimism. The skill with which I'd learned to smother any apprehensions almost as soon as they arose I'd learned from him as well. Tall and sturdy, his black hair combed back as if facing a perpetually strong wind, he was in charge of motion, the skipper of the ship of our family. His hazel eyes never stayed still, his gaze darting from the horizon to his feet and back, keeping pace with the flow of his thoughts, never at rest, always recalibrating our course, refiguring the most efficient way to get from here to there. So thoroughly did I adopt his billowing self-assurance, which could easily be mistaken for smugness, and his belief in the future—in the inevitable triumph of good sense and good intentions—that I feel as if the words I wrote were actually his, he the ventriloquist, me the obliging dummy on his knee.

Missing from these passages and others surrounding them is my signature anxiety, a tentativeness and occasional paralyzing immobility, which today, as for the past thirty years, hovers over nearly every act I contemplate. Should I wear lipstick to the luncheon at which I'll meet a new editor? Should I speak to my son's teacher when I pass her in the hall or wait till our scheduled conference? The questions multiply, sprouting new particulars like the Hydra, yet at bottom there is only one question: How can I make myself acceptable?

In 1964, when I was twelve, this question hadn't yet occurred to me.

What happened to the person who so assiduously kept this diary? I wonder, staring at the blank screen on my computer. I'd begun eighth grade as a surefooted, athletic girl barely able to contain her ambition; science was my favorite subject and sports a passion. Nine months later, school having eclipsed home in importance, in the amount of attention I devoted to studying and considering it, I loathed science and gym, I had turned klutzy on the softball field, and I'd decided to become a writer.

"Long, skinny, funny-looking (real cute)," was how I described a doll my parents had bought for me at F.A.O. Schwarz; reading the January 1964 entry now, I realize it's an inadvertent self-portrait of both my fantasy and my actual selves. The doll had a button nose, rouged cheeks, and the straight blond hair, coiffed in a perfect pageboy, that I, with my short, Brillo-y, brownish hair, couldn't help but covet. Her short, tented dress was red velvet, a color and fabric that I longed to see in my own wardrobe.

But the doll's most striking feature—and mine—was

her gangly legs, three or four times the length of her torso. They were spongy and could be bent and twisted—were capable, in other words, of all kinds of motion, if only her oversized feet hadn't been glued to the wooden pedestal. Yet I never viewed her as imprisoned. For years this doll, with its petite girl's torso supported by thick, boyish, athletic legs, stood on my desk—the perfect amalgam of how I saw myself and how I wished I would be seen.

Why, at this juncture of my life, do I feel compelled to return to this younger self, to dwell on events that happened thirty years ago? It is related, I'm sure, to my newfound freedom, to Ben's impending adolescence, and to my father's premature death, but in ways I can't yet understand.

For answers, I'll have to read the diary of my eighth-grade year, from the first day to the last, and see what secrets it yields.

It isn't an easy read. Though I'd made a great show each night of locking the volume with the tiny bronze key and burying both items at the bottom of my underwear drawer, where they wouldn't tempt either my mother or my sister, I'd known with prescient certainty that privacy, confidentiality, and ultimately honesty were all illusory. Even when I thought I was writing from my heart, I often wasn't. The very act of trying to encapsulate miasmic emotions into skinny, flat words is one of neither transcription nor even translation; it's a wholly other process, more like a Rube Goldberg contraption whereby a feeling flips a switch that pulls a trigger that moves a stylus on a piece of paper: the resulting squiggle isn't the feeling but merely represents it, issues from it in a maddeningly inexact way.

To think of a diary as a place where you can pour out your heart is to deceive yourself. Eventually it dawns on just about everyone who embarks on journal-keeping that words don't travel from heart to pen; they must first pass through the sentinel of your mind, a censor nearly as strict as one who cuts into Swiss cheese letters written to and from political prisoners. "My sister is such a bitch," I'd written in one of my earliest diaries, only to cross out the offending word—couldn't think it, certainly shouldn't write it.

For what if one day she read it? What if my children did? What would they think of me? Even worse was to imagine the fate of the diary after death had rendered me mute, unable to explain myself, to put my words in measured context. No one who keeps a copy of a letter or a record of her days doesn't worry about the posthumous fate of her words. "Burn all papers," we indelibly etch on the inside covers of our notebooks, diaries, and files, praying that our husbands, siblings, children, will respect this final gothic wish, praying that they won't.

We simultaneously crave privacy and exposure; this is the contradiction coiled at the heart of journal writing. Everything penned is meant to be read; every diarykeeper, no matter how old or how naive, posits an audience. We write to express all the things we fear to say lest we find ourselves rejected, while hoping that someone will one day rifle through these protected pages and murmur, "Oh, you poor baby, if only I'd known how you were feeling . . ."

At moments, rereading my diary, I want to hug the girl I was and comfort her in all her indecision and confusion; a page or two later, she infuriates me and makes me cringe. My reactions to what I wrote are as labile as the teenage moods that produced the words; like my newly adolescent son, I find myself laughing one second and crying the next, my emotions blending into each other the way radio stations swell in and out of range on a night when reception is bad.

Recording the present, re-creating the past, imagining the future—all are acts of approximation, of conjuring. The project I've launched, to understand what happened during eighth grade, becomes more of a dialogue than a journey. Gradually I realize that the cycle I feel I am ending didn't begin twelve years ago when I became a mother, as I assumed; in fact, bearing children was its apogee, not its inception. The cycle began thirty years ago, when I was twelve, the year I began eighth grade, a year of opportunity and danger prefiguring the one I now face, a year of enormous loss counterbalanced by commensurate gain, a year of choices whose consequences are still reverberating.

FIRST DAY

"As you all know," said Mr. Philip Black, his lizard-thin eyes gleaming as he paced back and forth in front of the classroom on gum-soled shoes, "this is an election year." Short and squat, nearly gnomish, with a low waist and center of gravity, he spoke gravely, as if dispensing information whose critical importance we would realize only in retrospect. At any moment I half expected to see his tongue dart from between his thin lips and snare an unsuspecting insect. It was September 10, 1964—the first day of eighth grade.

Back and forth he paced—his head down as if a stiff wind were emanating from the green chalkboard—from one end of the room to the other, pausing briefly to look out the window overlooking the parking lot, tossing a piece of chalk in his hand like a gangster with a silver dollar, cupping it and letting it go. Sometimes he stopped at his desk to put his foot up on his chair, cock his elbow on his knee, and rest his face in his palm. But not for long. He liked to walk, daring those of us ignorant enough to think he didn't have eyes in the back and sides of his head to act up. He wore white button-down shirts without ties, and dark slacks. His hair was salted with gray, and he had a pointy little beard that made him look not a little like the Devil.

He was a legend in the cit. ed. department, which stood for "citizenship education," my guidance counselor had explained to me. Back in Queens, where I began junior high school, we had called it "social studies," and it was often taught by English teachers. Here it had its own department, of which Mr. Black, though not chairman, was *genius loci.*

"You'll be responsible for much more work than you're used to," he said, full of bravado, a slightly sadistic smile playing around his lips. First he presented us with a verbal preview of the syllabus—we'd be assigned five reaction papers, a journal about the election, weekly essay tests, surprise quizzes. After each item he'd look up, just for a second, to calibrate our increasing dismay and fright. Then he went on, improvising new assignments on the spot, I felt sure, the way a coach slides new weights onto a barbell until the trainee can't budge it.

"Eighth grade is important," he continued, "because ninth grade is the first year of high school. Your grades count now. They matter. In a few years you'll take a test called the PSAT. What you get on that test will determine what college you go to. . . ."

Tension rose in the air like steam. Tests for college? I hadn't known anything about this. He smiled triumphantly to see the last holdouts among us pale. He was a terrorist, and he'd accomplished his goal—even I was scared. Yet my twelve-year-old fear was not paralytic, but almost arousing, nudging me into a state that approached what I now identify as sexual excitement. I could scarcely sit still. Bring on the work; I'd meet his challenge. I knew how to please men. It wasn't all that difficult.

"Your first long-range assignment," said Mr. Black, walking now between the rows of desks, "is to begin compiling a campaign journal. Everyone in the first two rows, you'll follow Johnson. The back two rows are responsible for Goldwater. Find an article in the newspaper every day about your candidate. Clip it. Paste it on a piece of paper. Underline the important passages. And write up a brief commentary."

Sitting in the back, as I always did because of my height, I found myself in Goldwater territory, which didn't thrill me. I considered myself opposed to everything he stood for.

"You have a problem with this assignment?" Mr. Black was standing directly in front of my desk.

"I just wish I'd gotten Johnson," I said.

"This will be more of a challenge." His flashing eyes stared deep into mine.

"I don't mind a challenge," I replied. The rest of the class tittered. They knew me better than he did.

I'd arrived at the school just six months earlier, on March 31, 1964, two days after my family had moved from our four-room apartment in Bayside to a ranch house on a quarter acre in eastern Nassau County. The junior high school, tucked away into a housing development near the intersection of two new highways, one heading north to the Sound and the other east to potato fields, was a short walk from my house. To my city-wise eyes, it looked like a movie-set school—miniaturized, underpopulated, and unnaturally calm.

On my first day of school, my mother and I met with Mrs. Eisen, my guidance counselor. Plump and gray-haired, she wore enormous red-framed glasses and a dress with peach and pink flowers. "Your records from Queens haven't yet arrived," she said, removing her glasses and nibbling on the earpiece.

Haven't arrived? My mother and I exchanged glances. Without my grades and scores, they didn't know who I was! I was a blank, a nobody! I felt naked, almost embarrassed. But slowly I began to realize what an opportunity was presenting itself to me. If they didn't know what to expect of me, they'd be amazed to see what a perfect student I could be.

Flustered, Mrs. Eisen began explaining that I'd be tracked for all my academic subjects, track 1 being the equivalent of honor classes. According to this system, each student had her own schedule card, and the deck was reshuffled for each class. In Queens, classes had traveled as herds. "We'll put you in all track 2 classes until your records arrive," Mrs. Eisen concluded.

For a moment I toyed with the notion of telling her that

she could save herself the trouble. But I didn't. I simply smiled and agreed, amazing even my mother.

Mrs. Eisen made a phone call, and a girl named Carol showed up a moment later to take me to my first class. I said to myself, with all sincerity, "Let them put me in whatever class they want. I know who I am, and soon they will too. The last laugh will be mine."

"School tomorrow," I'd written in my diary the previous night. "What if the girls are all tramps?"

Carol didn't seem at all like a tramp: she had kind, smiling eyes and touched my arm to steer me up the stairs, talking all the while. By the time we reached the track 2 cit. ed. class, I knew that she had an older and a younger brother, that her father had just begun medical school, and that Mr. Chesler, our cit. ed. teacher, was the cutest in the school. He was cute, I had to admit, cuter than any male teacher I'd had in Queens, but the next day, when Mrs. Eisen called me out of class and handed me a new schedule, rerouting me to track 1 classes, I left Mr. Chesler behind without a second thought. My records from Queens had arrived and, with them, vindication.

How Carol felt about my desertion, how my new classmates regarded me when I got the highest score on a surprise quiz given the first day I appeared, were questions I never asked myself. That what I did or how I acted had an impact on others didn't enter my mind. Nothing entered my mind, in fact, except the importance of making myself *known*. Sure, I wanted to be liked, to make new friends. But the way to accomplish this, it seemed to me, was to declare who I was. And I was a girl who not only did well in school but wanted to be known as such. To examine this as a tactic, to ponder whether this was the right way to go about endearing myself, never occurred to me. School was my Olympics, and I was bent on the gold.

"None of you should be afraid of trying," Mr. Black continued. "I have a daughter in eighth grade, and I tell her the same thing I'm about to tell you."

Here he paused for dramatic effect, sitting on his desk and facing us for the first time since class began. I must have smiled then, or shifted in my seat, or done something that made him stop pacing, consult his roster, and look directly at me. We locked eyes. Yes, I realized, this entire challenge is directed at me. Maybe he imagined himself talking to his daughter, just as I imagined him my father, talking to me. Somehow he'd managed to peer beneath my skin, to see me as I really was.

The bell signaling class change rang; Mr. Black kept us in our seats with his gaze alone. "You'll finish this year a different person than you began," he said, more prophet now than terrorist. What he meant, I assumed, was that come June we'd find ourselves more serious, more responsible, better informed—and that this change would be accomplished in an orderly, linear fashion and would prove all and only to the good.

"No one," he told us, stationed at the door, as we filed out of his classroom, to personally inspect each of us and issue his parting shot, "has ever gotten an *A* on one of my reaction papers. And I've been teaching for twenty years." At this point I walked past him, and he smiled. "No one."

Released from class, with a scant five minutes to arrive at the next, we burst forth, an eddying mob, a cacophonous herd, a coursing river of hormone-powered teenagers. We clogged the stairwells and hallways, shouting urgent messages to each other, passing notes, trading lunches.

Though the school was named for a citizen of local prominence, its motif was outer space. Each grade was housed in one of three two-story wings, named after Glenn, Grissom, and Shepard; "Aim High" was the school motto, *The Capsule* its newspaper; and on the athletic fields we cheered for our Astronauts. From an aerial view, I now realize, our school probably resembled a spaceship, the main office and auditorium up front, where the building tapered, forming the nose cone, the three squat academic wings out back the sturdy engines.

And we, the students, were the liquid fuel, the combustible force that circulated every forty-five minutes, generating enough energy to make the ground shake, the school vibrate, becoming very nearly airborne. It was as if the national preoccupation with space—with thrust, optimism, brute force overcoming all obstacles—echoed natural adolescence, so that each was intensified, amplified.

"The bell! The bell" we all shrieked when it caught us

unawares. Teachers appeared in doorways, shooing us, like items in a messy bedroom, into the bulging closet of our classrooms, forcing us into seats while they pressed their backs against the doors in relief. Squealing and snickering, we looked around to see where we had landed, which of our friends were in class with us, and who, finally, was our teacher.

After Mr. Black, anyone would have seemed anticlimactic. But no one more so than Mrs. Jane Johnson.

In retrospect I realize she must have been in her mid to late forties. At the time, my friends and I never spent a moment calculating her age. From the three-piece patterned dresses, the faux-pearl earrings and gold-tone bracelets, the lipstick, which always flaked off, and the short, hennaed hair that framed her face in frizzy little curls, we assumed, tacitly, that she was older than our mothers and younger than our grandmothers.

Yet she wasn't home, like our mothers and grandmothers, but was teaching honors English.

I felt like crying, like bolting from the room. She was a throwback, as traditional a teacher as I'd ever encountered, right down to her fussy, meticulously slanted handwriting, the glasses on a chain around her neck, and her schoolmarm's distracted air of thinking of something else while managing the class. An elementary-school teacher just like the ones I'd outgrown. My mother's idea of an English teacher.

I filled out Delaney cards on which teachers kept track of our attendance, scanned the mimeographed syllabus, studied with dismay the piles of books placed around the room, the sweat induced by Mr. Black barely dry on my back. If his class was a roller coaster, English was standing in line for tickets.

Just look at this syllabus. *Johnny Tremain* was the first book we'd read. Each week, there would be a writing assignment to be done in class, completed at home, turned in for editing, and then rewritten. We'd also work on creative writing, Mrs. Johnson said, fingering her necklace, aligning the corners of papers on her desk, though at first we'd write the endings to stories, eventually working up to stories of our own. We'd also read plays. And poetry. Haiku.

Everyone groaned. My friend Beth, seated behind me, kicked my chair. Alice, a girl I'd hated on first sight, was sitting next to me; she rolled her eyes and sighed. Last year she'd shown up at the seventh-grade dance in an off-the-shoulder screaming red chiffon dress and high heels, while I clumped around the gym in a white-and-brown checked dress sporting a big white collar that in my bedroom mirror had looked very chic but had begun to smell inexplicably of fish. Now she smiled, and I smiled back.

Behind her sat Denise, who'd been to elementary school with Alice. She had a deep, infectious laugh and a spidery handwriting that I loved. Nearby sat Anna, a dark-haired, endearing girl from my neighborhood who had graciously walked home from school with me on my first day and had done so ever since. And in the back, near the window, leaning back on his chair, sat dark-haired, wiry

Rod, a boy I'd long had my eye on. Eddie, who'd been in classes with me the year before, was stationed near the door. It was very nearly a party.

And we were all in agreement—this class was deadly. Reading and writing, I thought: how ridiculous that these could be construed as a subject. These activities were part of life's infrastructure, things I did all the time, without thinking about them. English wasn't a "subject," not in the same way math or French or even history was a subject that had to be tackled, studied, mastered, tested. Taking it completely for granted, I thought about English all the time and not at all. I had nothing to prove in the class, because there was clearly nothing to teach and nothing to learn.

"But we won't start poetry until after the holidays," Mrs. Johnson said. There was something unflappable about her. She didn't seem to notice that English was no one's favorite subject, that she had less total charisma than Mr. Black had in his eyebrows. Her class had no present; it would be as timeless and musty as the classics we'd be reading. She didn't once mention the upcoming election or college boards—she spoke of nothing but books and writing.

We did get an assignment before the bell rang and released us: to write a single paragraph about a mistake we'd made.

By third period, the spaceship of our school seemed to be leaking energy. Mrs. Villard, my math teacher, didn't even get up as we filed into her classroom. She sat behind her desk with a sweater draped over her shoulders, greeting each of us with a benign but distant smile, nodding as we took our seats. When the bell rang, she began talking, and she sat throughout the entire period, rising only to write things on the board.

Older than Mrs. Johnson, she was taller and almost painfully thin. Her hair, miraculously, had no color. She spoke firmly but flatly.

About what? I have virtually no memory of the first day of this class. She didn't proselytize, didn't attempt to convince us, as my father occasionally did, that one day math would come to our rescue, that we'd need to remember how to find a square root or the circumference of a circle.

She didn't wax poetic about the beauty of math, about how it was a language all its own. Whatever energized Mrs. Villard, it didn't seem to have anything to do with numbers or children. Why was she here?

Why was *I* here? Looking around the hushed room, I realized that I knew almost no one.

Interestingly, math was the only subject in which I hadn't been switched from track 2 to track 1 after my records arrived. I'm not sure why. I'd always done well enough in math, my average hovering around 90. It was never my favorite subject, simply one I knew I needed to master if I intended to become an archaeologist or a medical researcher. Understanding had always seemed just a breath away.

But in Mrs. Villard's class I felt more lonely than hopeful, surrounded by kids I recognized from the gym, my homeroom, and the neighborhood, but with whom I rarely spoke. They were as surprised to see me as I was to see them.

Mrs. Villard was surprised by nothing. She took attendance, closed her roll book, and opened her math book. She regarded us as impassively as she would have a study hall class, a random collection of students toward whom she had no greater obligation than to keep order.

The minutes crept by. I studied the clock and wondered if all track 2 classes were like this. With my eyes open, I settled in for a forty-five-minute snooze.

Mrs. Villard's polar opposite, her very antithesis, was Mme. Rizzoli, who taught the most frenetic French class I'd ever sat through. She chattered away, exclusively in French, from the moment we entered the room until after the bell rang, the way people who can't stand silence talk incessantly.

Like a petite tropical bird, she stood behind her desk, the tips of her fingers touching the surface as if she were just the slightest bit tipsy and needed help balancing. Her skirt was voluminous, long, and brightly colored in a mad, patternless print, and she wore light-green ballet-type shoes to match.

Though she stood still, her voice trilled up and down the room, from window to door, from ceiling to floor, with a fluid outpouring of questions, comments, exhortations, reminders—all in a gush of French.

This year, we'd continue with the method we'd used the year before: dialogues to memorize, stories about Papa taking us to the museum, and eating *saucisson* on *mercredi;* enfolded within these contrived conversations were not only lessons on the use of the subjunctive and past particles but also tidbits of French culture—the fact, for example, that French students stayed home on Thursdays. Once a week we'd devote an entire class to nonlanguage matters: the geography of Paris, the Eiffel Tower, that lace was made in Cluny, and that Lyon is known for its cuisine.

Only Denise was in class with me; Alice and Beth had opted for Spanish, which had been deemed the more "useful" language. French exerted a certain resistance to the world around us, a stubborn insistence that despite its patent impracticality, it was too lovely to ignore.

French, like math, was for me a second-tier subject, a subject in which there was no struggle, no tension. And virtually no hope. I'd never sound like Mme. Rizzoli, no matter had hard I tried, no matter how much I pretended—when I sang French songs to myself or practiced my dialogues in private—that I did.

"Is she French, or Italian?" Denise asked me in a note. I shrugged. What did it matter? As Mme. Rizzoli wrote our assignment on the board, I tried to figure out how she fixed her hair, where the thick reddish-brown braid began, where she cinched it, how she pinned it to her scalp. And all the while, she kept talking, and growing more and more remote.

Sometime during third period, the aromas of institutional cooking—dry hot dogs, caked navy bean soup—came wafting through the halls, slipping under the doors of closed classrooms, whispering of release.

Lunch was served over the three middle periods of the day. From all corners of the school we'd swoop into the cafeteria, located at the front of the building, the nose cone of our rocket ship, facing the athletic fields and the Long Island Expressway, with its incessant current of traffic. To the cafeteria workers and aides, we must have seemed like atoms in a reactor chamber subjected to intense heat, condemned to zip around the room in chaotic motion.

It was nothing short of ear-splitting bedlam, and I was lost. The previous year, I'd eaten my lunch each day with Maureen, a girl who lived around the corner from me and was mildly retarded, quite simply because she was the first familiar face I saw when I took my initial tentative steps into the cafeteria. She sat near the door, sparing herself a walk past countless tables, and looked so happy and grateful when I sat down across from her that I made a habit of it. We barely talked. She ate with her mouth open, smiling apologetically. I kept my head down, read when I was finished, and found the arrangement quite satisfactory.

But this year, I knew instinctively that this wouldn't do. The moment I saw Maureen at our regular table, looking hopefully toward me, I pretended not to see her. Someone called my name—Alice, from English. She was sitting with others I recognized from the class—popular girls, who had danced with boys at the seventh-grade dance—and waved me over.

Now I was the one to feel grateful and relieved. I dug out the sandwich I'd brought from home, squashed and misshapen. No one else was eating. Their sandwich bags sat on the table, untouched.

Conversation swirled around me, punctuated by convulsive laughter, blushing, books slammed on tables. I knew only some of the people being talked about. Boys. Teachers. Movie actors. A boy from my science class walked by with a cafeteria tray—those who bought hot lunches were faintly derided; their mothers worked and couldn't pack them lunch—and set all the girls at the table into gales of laughter. They clamped their hands over their mouths to muffle screams. They played with their hair. They blew up at each other and five seconds later apologized. They laughed uproariously until they choked and had to be pounded on the back, everything an excuse for histrionics.

In short, it was a frenzy—a caricature—of connectedness, a riot of relatedness that used up kilowatts of energy but left us energized, not depleted, a raucous back-and-forth, she-said-but-what-she-really-meant-was, where every conversation, every look, was scavenged for meaning and innuendo. I couldn't begin to keep up.

When the warning bell rang, everyone screamed and

grabbed a soggy sandwich to either eat, trade, or throw away. Lunch was almost over. Three more periods to get through.

I tried to eat so no one would notice me. It was a place without order, without rules or expectations. There were no assignments to fulfill, no way to get noticed except through means I couldn't imagine. The orderliness of classes, of the teacher-student relationship, was something I clung to. This was pure emotional chaos. And I harbored a terrible secret: of all those hundreds of children, I was the only one who couldn't wait for the bell to ring, couldn't wait to get back to class.

The most breathtaking fact about science was Miss Delray's tininess. She was the smallest adult any of us had ever seen. Her stick straight red hair was cut close to her head. She dressed well, though in what children's department she shopped we couldn't imagine. Everything about her was diminutive, save for an outsized opal ring she wore on the middle finger of her right hand.

Why wasn't she married?

Calling the roll, she pronounced our names with a quiet yet commanding intensity, studying each syllable like a scientific formula, looking up to scrutinize our faces, affixing name to face and then privately smiling as if at some implicit punch line. Sometimes she actually chuckled, a sound produced so far back in her throat that little sound actually emerged; you read her laughter mostly in her dark eyes.

Without consulting notes, she began explaining the year's syllabus, speaking slowly, as if she'd never allow herself to rush through a sentence before carefully parsing it in her head. We'd be doing actual experiments this year, she informed us, taking what was for her a huge step up to the black lab table at the front of the room and pointing out the sinks, spigots, jets, the drawers of beakers and pipettes. Each of these objects she fingered in a slow, languorous way, as if the objects, their shapes and textures, brought her pleasure. It seemed odd, unseemly, inappropriate, as if she were demonstrating a fetish.

"I want you each to come up here, one by one," she announced, "to stand behind the desk and see all the equipment." Positioned near the door, she greeted us like a hostess on a receiving line. Next to her I felt enormous, unformed, and klutzy.

Maybe I was nonplussed by the fact that she was a woman. All my previous science teachers, from my father on, had been men, of a specific mold—tall and energetic, equal parts theoretician and tinkerer, able not only to understand the world but to manipulate it, improve upon it: create miniature volcanoes, build birdhouses, bookshelves, toy chests, and lamps.

But Miss Delray was cut from different cloth. Her room was pathologically neat and organized, just like her person. I couldn't divine her attitude toward science or anything else, save for a general tone of ironic watchfulness. When the bell cut her off midsentence, she smiled wistfully and shrugged. She knew she'd see us tomorrow.

• • •

Those of us who didn't play an instrument in school found ourselves in chorus, which met in the band room, across the hall from the boys' gym. At the podium stood Mr. Eli Hammer. He wasn't at all good looking, nor was he particularly friendly, but just by dint of being young and having blond hair and blue eyes, he became an object of desire and speculation. In fact, he reminded me of the very boys whom he scolded with vague threats and withering looks; it couldn't have been that long since he himself was sitting in the back of a music room, smirking.

There was something off-kilter about being in chorus. The girls badly outnumbered the boys, yet the handful of tenors and even fewer basses had center stage, positioned directly in front of Mr. Hammer, sopranos and altos flanking them like bookends.

My friend Ilene, the accompanist, positioned her upright piano near the soprano section so she could take part in the conversations that no amount of shushing by Mr. Hammer completely extinguished. At the piano she was transformed: she sat perfectly erect, her impossibly agile fingers on the keys, one eye on Mr. Hammer, one on the music, ready for an upbeat.

Alternating with chorus was art, the deadest party of the day. We sat in groups of four on high metal chairs at paint-splattered tables while Miss Castro, who had the blondest hair I'd ever seen, opened cabinet after cabinet, pointing out all the supplies we'd be using: pipe cleaners, acrylics, glitter, oak tag, markers in every color. She was practically salivating as she fingered the papers, studied the colors, ran her hands over the different textures and surfaces.

None of my friends were in my class. If I had been pressed to name my favorite color, I wouldn't have been able to decide between blue and red. Art was a more foreign language to me than French. At least there were no tests. All I had to do was show up and try not to get my hands dirty.

What a joke—the home ec teacher was named Mrs. Cooke! And look at this room, my friends and I said to each other, trying to settle down after the bell rang. Not only was it set up with three miniature kitchens, like a dollhouse, but Mrs. Cooke resembled the mom we saw on commercials, who put on a dress to make breakfast, her hair coiffed and her nails manicured. She was tall and thin and fair-haired, a whirlwind of efficiency who could cook up a meal and sew up a dress without breaking a sweat.

The period was sexualized because classes were segregated; the boys, off in the shop with the burly shop teacher, whose apron was always full of grease, were gone. No snickering from the back of the room. No distractions.

Yet the class was terrifying in its single-mindedness. "By the end of the year," Mrs. Cooke told us, smiling brightly, "you'll be responsible for serving a meal to the rest of the class and for creating a dress you'll model at the fashion show out on the patio."

In her own way, Mrs. Cooke had expectations as terrifying as Mr. Black's, yet hers induced paralysis rather than its opposite. I'd never, *never* succeed in this class. "I hate linen and dishes and all that crap," I'd recently written in my diary, an entry prompted by my mother's attempts to teach me how to wash dishes properly.

We all felt imprisoned by home ec, face-to-face with our shortcomings. Mrs. Cooke didn't notice. She demonstrated her machines, her appliances, the conveniences to which we'd be exposed, as if she couldn't have been more pleased. Untying her apron and hanging it on a hook, she gave us our homework assignment: buy muslin with which to make an apron, and bring it to class with a spool of matching thread.

Last period. The gym teachers, Mrs. Cooper and Miss Smith, knew us all from the previous year. Nonetheless, we convened in the locker room for the start-of-school speech and were issued blue gym suits, one-piece numbers in royal blue, which, despite a thousand snaps, managed to fit no one properly.

"Get your name on the pocket," Mrs. Cooper said, studying her nails, "and don't forget it at home." Her sparse hair was dyed jet black, and some of the dye had mistakenly been applied to her scalp. She had long, pointy, fire-engine-red fingernails, and all the bones in her arms and legs stood out, as if in bas-relief. Miss Smith, on the other hand, had a doughy body, short and squat, with no apparent backbone. They were the Mutt and Jeff of physical education: together, the ectomorphic Mrs. Cooper and the roly-poly Miss Smith made one human being of normal consistency, size, and shape.

"We'll start with tennis," Miss Smith began. "Then, when it's too cold to play outside, volleyball, dodgeball, and gymnastics. Modern dance. Health. Softball." The usual list. Only health was new.

"That's it for today," Mrs. Cooper said, looking toward her office, where a cup of coffee with serious lipstick stains sat on her desk and a cigarette burned in an ashtray. "Oh, yes"—she called us back. "One more thing, girls. Don't forget the deodorant."

FALL

SEPTEMBER 17:

I'm dead tired. Homework in every subject and tons of tests. Math quiz was easy, French quiz tomorrow. Elected to student council. I'm doing lousy in science. Yanks won—first place! Mick—200th hit! So happy!!!

P.S. Watch Beatles—7:00, channel 7.

Wasting no time, on the second day of class Mr. Black announced that we'd spend the next several weeks learning about the history and structure of government since the Greeks.

Lamblike, we sat at our desks and took notes. There was nothing to discuss; we merely listened and copied down what he said, in outline form. If I paused to gaze out the window, study what the girl next to me was wearing, or glance at the clock, I'd find myself hopelessly lost when I tuned back in. The period flew by, and we all left the room shaking our writing hand to loosen it up. This wasn't school as much as intellectual boot camp. We were being drilled to see how much material we could absorb, how long we could endure.

By the time we found ourselves in English, we were exhausted. Forty-five minutes with Mrs. Johnson felt unnaturally protracted. She spoke, moved, and wrote on the blackboard with excruciating deliberation, her walk-before-you-run attitude leaving us feeling as if time were standing still.

"Where oh where is our Mr. Loehman?" I wrote on a

piece of paper, which I then folded into a tidy triangular packet and palmed to my friend Beth, sitting behind me, while Mrs. Johnson droned on about the importance of writing a *single* paragraph before moving on to an essay.

Beth kicked my chair in response. Mr. Loehman, the English teacher we both had last year, impossibly young and cute and unorthodox, had bolted—had he been fired?—leaving teaching and Long Island behind. Beth and I were the only ones who missed him.

In his class, English had come alive. We'd studied advertising and propaganda, debated politics and written editorials. Now we were supposed to think about a single paragraph? We were supposed to care about books written decades ago? This was time travel backward, into the dim and boring past.

For Mrs. Johnson's first assignment, to write about a mistake we'd made, I'd concocted a paragraph in a heavy-handed, self-mocking tone about a tantrum I had thrown when my parents told me that we were moving. I'd titled it "Wrong Again."

Mrs. Johnson pointed out a few spelling and pronoun-placement errors, wrote a sentence or two about its readability, and gave me an 85—a low grade for me, but at least I had the last laugh. The paragraph was a total lie; I'd made up the entire incident.

And she didn't even know! Mr. Loehman would have sniffed out my dishonesty, I was sure. I missed him terribly—and not for the obvious reason, that he had been, according to Carol, my first-day guide, the cutest teacher in school after Mr. Chesler.

What she had meant, I realized after a few periods in his class, was that his thick, blunt-cut wedge of auburn hair made him resemble a Beatle, though we never agreed on which one, and that he was very young, though how young—scarcely a decade older than we were—escaped us.

He owed his reputation to those girls, like Carol, who simply passed him in the hall, not those who sat in his classroom and scrutinized him. Up close, his face was more rugged than Mr. Chesler's, too craggy for real cuteness. His clothes were at first intriguing—sports jacket, khaki trousers, knit ties, slightly scuffed black work shoes—but ultimately proved too casual. By the time I entered the class, in March, a certain disillusionment had set in among the other girls, as if he hadn't quite lived up to his original promise.

"We're talking about advertising," he said when I walked into the room and sat down, as if I'd been absent for a week and needed filling in rather than welcoming. There was nothing teacherly about him, not as I knew teachers. He didn't take command of a room the way other male teachers did, nor was he fussy and prim; rather, he looked like someone surprised to find himself hired for a job he'd had no original intention of taking. In fact, it was his first—and last—year teaching in a public junior high.

"An experiment was conducted in a movie theater," he explained. "Before the movie started, the words 'Buy popcorn' flashed on the screen for a fraction of a second. Too short a time for anyone to actually read them. No one noticed it. But popcorn sales in the lobby increased nearly one hundred percent. This is called subliminal advertising. Think of the implications."

It wasn't so much an order as an invitation: Think with me, he seemed to be saying, sitting on the front of the desk, his thick-soled shoes gently swaying. He wanted to know what we thought.

Silence hung uneasily in the room. Some students stared back, unembarrassed by having nothing to say. Others yawned.

"I like the things he talks about," I wrote in my diary, after only two days in his class. But the fact that Beth and I were the only ones who felt this way was becoming distressingly clear to us all.

He asked us to bring in a magazine or newspaper advertisement that caught our eye. The Marlboro Man provoked him; we spent several periods dissecting his appeal. "What is this ad trying to say to you? What is it appealing to inside you?" he'd ask, relentlessly, and I had the experience, for the first time, of trying to put into words something I'd never before talked about.

One afternoon we segued from an advertisement to politics, and found ourselves in the midst of a unit on propaganda. In other classes, a new unit meant turning the page in your loose-leaf and writing a heading, opening to a new chapter in the textbook. But Mr. Loehman simply sat down on the edge of the desk, loosened his already loose tie, and began talking. The Cold War was at its apogee; we were all aware of the ways in which the Communists manipulated words for their own purposes. I volunteered to subscribe to the *Daily Worker,* which arrived each month in its brown wrapper, and brought it into class for inspection.

But wait a minute, he said suddenly one day, what about the Pledge of Allegiance? Isn't that also propaganda? What does patriotism mean? he asked us. *Is* there liberty and justice for all?

I felt adrift during this class, dizzy when I left, unable to put the Pledge and propaganda into the same category. Write a new pledge, which has meaning, he said. What he was really asking us, of course, was to examine the basic underpinnings of our life, to empty our dresser drawers of all the intimate little folded objects we'd mindlessly acquired and stashed away, to hold each one up to the bright light of day and then very clearly say, Yes, I need this, or No, I don't.

He didn't seem to care much about anything else, which is not to say he didn't notice. He knew, I assumed, the extent to which he mystified, intrigued, disoriented, and captivated me, the degree to which I attended to his every word, yet he treated me with the same aloof smile he bestowed on the scoffing boys and girls in the back, the ones who complained to their parents, their friends, their guidance counselors. Each paper I handed in was judged on its merits, not on how trenchantly I had analyzed the previous assignment. He treated me as neither a girl nor a boy, simply as a mind that needed to be cracked. When I proudly told him that I'd bought myself a desk plaque that stated, "Protest against the rising tide of conformity," he smiled wanly, allowing me to realize in a flash the depth of my foolishness in succumbing to a commercial version of a tenet he held dear.

No grades, no red pen—he used green ink and printed with such force that the letters were palpable—no tests, no reports, no dittos, no due dates: it wasn't much of an English class. No one was really surprised when he announced, on the day of our final, that he wouldn't be returning in the fall. We already knew of his battles with guidance counselors, the administration, parents who objected to their children's reading communist newspapers, and students who wanted grades and test scores. Even Mrs. Eisen, who had championed him to me, who had beamed as she penciled his name on my schedule on my second day of school, had called him in for a talk, hoping to set him straight. He knew most of us would soon forget him. Still, he wrote his address on the board and said if anyone wrote to him he'd write back. I was the only one who copied it down. Our correspondence has lasted to this day.

Seventh-grade English, I realize now, was my personal introduction to the sixties. What gathered momentum throughout high school, was celebrated at Woodstock, and culminated at Kent State began with an avidity of questioning, with more than a willingness—an insistence—to examine everything that was handed down, that was assumed, taken on faith, taken for granted. Mr. Loehman wasn't trying to teach us but was inviting us to begin our own personal journey toward clear thinking, to tunnel us through the thick veneer of suburban slather to some kind of light. There's a world inside the world we see, was his message. Not everything reveals itself immediately. Be suspicious. Question everything.

But Mrs. Johnson asked no questions. Nothing provoked her. She didn't look beyond the subject matter to larger implications. She lacked both the stamina and inclination.

And Mr. Black brooked no questions. "On Thursday, October 7, you will have your first essay test," he abruptly announced one morning in late September, tossing a piece of chalk into the air and catching it in the same hand. "It will be on the material we've covered so far."

All the material? His pronouncement induced the precise reaction he'd hoped for: collective panic. His timing was perfect. True, he'd warned us that a test loomed in our future. But weeks had gone by without any further mention of an exam, and we'd come to think we'd been miraculously exempted.

"Ask some of my students from last year about my essay tests," he suggested. His eyes glinted. He couldn't help himself.

October 6:

I have such stupid friends. The test from Mr. Black—I studied enough so that I can repeat everything backwards. I ain't killing myself any more. I feel like an answering machine. Seven calls tonight, all about cit. ed. Only 2 essays. Hell! Worried.

I should have been worried. Announcement of the test made me realize I had nothing that resembled formal study habits. In the past, I'd simply read over the relevant material and gotten a good night's sleep. Clearly, that wouldn't do for Mr. Black.

The only strategy I could come up with involved rewriting all my class notes. At least I'd be doing something, and I'd have a sheaf of papers to show for my effort.

After dinner, I planted myself in an easy chair in the living room and began transcribing into paragraph form the outlined notes I took in class. I used the back, blank sides of an order pad my father had brought home from work, the front imprinted with thick black lines and columns that the employees he supervised filled in and submitted for his approval.

He sat across the room, lost in the *New York Times.* Occasionally he'd yawn, reach for some licorice, jiggle the newsprint pages on his knee to even them before folding the section and putting it down. His work was done for the day. Mine had only begun.

And what kind of work did he do, anyway? He didn't have an official title, like Alice's father, who was a sales manager; he didn't sell anything I could wear or take to school, like Ilene's father, who had a leather-coat store. He worked in an electronics company.

An ocean-lover, he'd sensed the swelling wave of post-war technology just as it began to gather energy far off-shore, and he'd majored in physics and engineering. His first job, which he held until I was about six, was with a Brooklyn company called Coilwinders—easy enough to imagine him winding coils, much the way my mother twirled her just-shampooed hair around her finger before pinning spit curls to her head with bobby pins.

A few years later, when he wanted a change, he flirted with taking a job at Grumman or one of the other stirring behemoths on Long Island, but he opted instead for a fledgling electronics company founded by two acquaintances in a Queens basement. Since then they'd moved to a hill in Glen Cove. "The shop" is what my father called the place where he worked, as if it were a dark, smelly sweatshop left over from his parents' generation rather than a brash, upstart company jockeying for position in a frontier full of unlimited promise.

I remember the frigid afternoon he drove us to the parcel of land on which the new factory was being built, the wind off the Sound whipping too fiercely over the vacant lot for my grandmother, mother, and sister to get out of the car. We were all in our weekend clothes. My father, who didn't have to dress up for work, groomed himself like a lawyer on weekends: sleek black coat, black leather gloves, and gray fedora. I wore a brown tweed coat trimmed in brown velvet and an itchy brown corduroy hat that tied under my chin. My mother, in Persian lamb, ventured from the snug cave of the car just long enough to coax my sister out for a snapshot: my father crouched on one knee on the frozen, rock-studded ground, one arm around each of his daughters, surveying the construction site, a bulldozer to the right, and behind us a water tower, which is all that today remains.

"That's where the main entrance will go, the shipping area, the machine shop," my father told my grandfather, a rotund man who rubbed his hands together—he never wore gloves—and nodded. I looked into the stinging wind, my eyes tearing, and tried to see into the future too.

I loved visiting the shop, when it was completed, and looked forward to those late Saturday afternoons when my father would need to drive there to pick up something he'd forgotten. We'd enter through the small office where the secretary and bookkeeper sat, an inelegant cubicle decorated with plastic flowers and Naugahyde couches, an engineer's afterthought. I'd play at the switchboard, open desk drawers to study the pens, take a drink from the water cooler.

A small door led to the back of the building, where my father worked, or, rather, presided. Here things were received, produced, forged, soldered, constructed, packaged, shipped. Grimy cartons and oily, unwieldy machinery lined the walls; scattered throughout were items

I recognized—the work order pads he brought home for scrap paper, thick pencils that you sharpened by unwinding a strip of paper from the point, blueprints on tables in his handwriting, his careful numbers, the eight a squat snowman.

Shortly after he died, the shop was sold to a larger local electronics company and eventually dissolved. He'd been uncomfortable at work the last few years; the front office had been transformed, softened, color-coordinated; men were hired who called it "the Company," with whom he'd disagreed over fundamental issues such as corporate direction. "Your father had a great organizational mind," one of his coworkers told me during the shiva call—the man with whom he had most often disagreed—and it dawned on me then that my father's recent work difficulties stemmed from the fact that he'd been an efficiency expert before the word had been coined and that he'd outlived his usefulness: the company no longer prized efficiency. He'd become an anachronism.

Though his had never been a desk job, he'd managed to keep his old-fashioned wooden desk through the plant's redecoration—when everything else was transformed into high-tech steel, gray and mauve—and a battered and creased high-backed brown chair that both reclined and swiveled. Like his car, the desk surface was spotless and orderly, though bereft of personal items like photos or mugs. One afternoon, left alone at his desk, I began rummaging through his drawers. Stashed behind the memo pads, pens, clips, fasteners, and tape, I found, to my surprise, what looked like a month's supply of Chiclets, a half-empty pack of Camels, an ashtray, and a pair of tortoiseshell eyeglasses. It was stunning, this discovery, that at work he was a totally different person, a person who chewed gum, wore glasses, smoked—things he never did when he was busy being my father. It was as if I'd stumbled upon his secret identity.

From my chair, I studied my father as much as my cit. ed. notes. Work—man's work—was mysterious and invisible. You persevered: woke up, fed the fish, put on work clothes, said good-bye to your family, returned in time for dinner, and expected results. And you succeeded, always. You made people proud of you. When you changed jobs, you stopped work at the old company on a Friday and began the new job on a Monday, without skipping a paycheck. When you went to school, you studied as hard as you could and brought home good grades. My father and Mr. Black, two men who had never met and looked nothing like each other, became my twin challengers and instant allies. Do us proud, they said. Don't fail us.

The morning after our essay test, Mr. Black hurried us into our seats. He'd rolled our test papers into a thin baton. Had he stayed up all night, grading them? "There was only one hundred," he said, "among both of my track 1 classes. That's pretty much what I've come to expect. The grades weren't bad over all. They could have been better." He began passing them out.

He placed each paper facedown on the desk. I turned mine over slowly. A red *100* at the top. No other comments. I looked up, to find him staring at me. I didn't look away. I knew he was seeing me exactly as my father did, as I saw myself—as someone lucky enough to be equal parts girl and boy, a social hermaphrodite.

"What'd you get?" people began asking me. Mr. Black, pretending he didn't hear, kept passing out the remaining papers. He was trying not to smile.

Beth, behind me, tapped me on the shoulder. My heart pounded, my palms were sweating. I took my test paper and held it up so she could see.

"You got a hundred?" she gasped, genuinely shocked. She turned her own paper over, saw her grade, and covered it with her hand.

"She got a hundred." The news spread through the room like an out-of-control game of telephone.

One hundred. A perfect grade. I'd done it. Mr. Black began talking about what the next test would cover, giving me, I was sure, a chance to savor my victory in private. That my friends and classmates might have felt a twinge of envy, that they might have been angry or resentful—as I felt toward them when they excelled—didn't occur to me. To be brutally frank, as Mr. Black used to say, I didn't think of them at all, except as my audience. The awareness of others' feelings is digital—you have it or you don't. Once you stumble upon it, there's no going back.

Like a child, I assumed that those around me were applauding my every move. At the front of the pack, I simply didn't turn around. Knowing full well that Mr. Black was stingy with praise—that his approbation of me meant that others went wanting—didn't dim the glory I was experiencing. My classmates' feelings, their very existences, wasn't something I thought about.

Beneath this was a simple, childlike strategy: the way to make and keep friends was less to approach individual girls than to excel, to position myself squarely in the spotlight. Then others would seek me out, would want to befriend me, and popularity would follow.

The buzz surrounding my good fortune hung in the air throughout the period. I was exhausted by the time the bell rang and eager for the anonymity of math.

"Hey, I heard you got a hundred on Black's test"—a boy I didn't know at all stopped me in the hall after English. During lunch, I learned that Mr. Black had told his other track 1 class about my grade. By day's end, it seemed as if the whole school knew.

"So how does it feel to be a star?" Alice asked me when we met at our lockers that afternoon.

How did I feel? As if I'd stepped up to bat in the lengthening shadows of Yankee Stadium during the last game of the World Series against St. Louis and hit a home run so towering that the ball was never recovered.

PHYS. ED.

I'd had an early education in competition. In our Bayside apartment building, just opposite the incinerator on our floor, lived a family with two boys—chubby, cheerful Freddy, a year older than I was, and his brother, Mike, my sister's age. Their apartment had only one bedroom and was much smaller than ours—the kitchen too small to hold a table—but their windows faced front, overlooking the crescent we lived on and the two moon-shaped parks flanking Seventy-fifth Avenue, one of which we knew as intimately as a backyard.

Freddy's mother and mine were friends; roughly equal in height and girth, they cultivated the art of talking so quietly that we could scarcely hear them. Freddy's father, Hank, was many inches shorter than mine, and sold insurance. Sometimes he came over to our apartment and talked to my father at the kitchen table. When he left, I could tell that my father was grateful he was not a salesman.

During the week, Freddy and I played well enough together, but on weekends, when our fathers were home, they became coaches and we reluctant competitors. We were never evenly matched, Freddy shorter and heavier than I was; these handicaps, however, were neutralized in our fathers' minds by the fact that he was a boy and I, despite my athleticism, was a girl.

Everything that you could do in a playground—swing, ride a bike, throw a ball—came more easily to me than to Freddy. Days after my training wheels came off, Freddy's came off too, but as I took solo laps around the playground's perimeter under my father's proud eye, Hank ran behind his son's bike, steadying the tottering seat, red-faced from the strain.

We had footraces too, staged by our fathers, from one end of the playground to the other, which I always won by several lengths. Did my father ever notice how Hank squatted and clapped his hands, both cheerleader and coach, willing his son along, hoping that just once Freddy would eke out a victory? Did my father notice Hank shifting his weight from side to side, breathing hard, as if he were the one running, his pinched smiled revealing surprise, disappointment, hope, and finally resignation when I won again? Or was my dad too busy beaming, a triumphant smile lighting his eyes, as if to say, "Who can blame me if I delight in my child?" He wasn't easily pleased, but when he succumbed he gave himself entirely over to pleasure, and I was often its source.

By the time Freddy crossed the finish line, Hank had turned away. Did my father feel a momentary pang to see his neighbor's evident pain? If he did, he didn't show it; nor did he let his knowledge of Hank's feelings spoil his own sense of victory. We always try our hardest, his unflinching smile told me; you always run flat out as if there's no tomorrow, as if everything has to be accomplished today, right now, every single time.

My mother had ice skates. Not white, like mine, with serrated front edges, but black with smooth blades. Hockey skates, she told me, from college. I saw them every time I went to the closet to get my own. She brought them with her on our trips to the ponds my father had scouted out—as a last resort we'd end up at a flooded and iced-over playground, never an indoor rink. But she usually stationed herself on the shore, snapping photos while my father, my sister, and I skated.

"What happened?" I wanted to ask, was on the verge of asking her, but never did. What changed? Why did she stop skating? Why didn't she play catch or tennis with me? She had a racket too. But her equipment gathered dust in the closet while she sat on the sidelines. It wasn't that she didn't like to skate anymore; I could see tucked away behind her eyes, at the corner of her mouth, that she remembered the giddy sensation of gliding, the sound and satisfying feel of blades cutting into ice, the frigid wintry air filling your chest with an oxygenated elation. She loved it. All she had to do was lace up her skates again. But she never did.

"We were going to name you Rutherford Schuyler," my father used to tell me. He never tired of the old family jokes—each repetition induced new peals of pleasure—and I seemed an especially satisfactory target.

"But what would you have *called* me?" I'd ask. The fact that the name lent itself to no nickname I knew of most concerned my young sensibility.

"Rutherford Schuyler," he'd deadpan. The joke, I thought, was in the name, which was both gentile and presidential; neither grandmother, try as she might, could successfully diminutize or Yiddishize it.

It was also a boy's name, of course, but so remote was it from my actual experience—from the names of any boys I knew—that I never said to myself, "He wishes he had a son." So astonishingly deft was my father's sleight of hand that it didn't occur to me until I was a grown woman that I was supposed to have been a boy named Robert.

It also obscured for me until many years later the crucial reality: that Rutherford Schuyler wasn't merely a family joke. The preposterous name hadn't been rejected, in favor of a more suitably feminine one, but had been bestowed, to help alleviate my father's sense of disappointment, which, however crushing, wasn't contagious—I wasn't disappointed in myself. I simply knew that in my father's eyes I was a boy.

This fiction, in which we all colluded, was by many lights well intentioned. My father, born only two generations out of Europe, could see plainly enough what happened to girls in his family. His mother, an imposing, strong-willed woman with a prodigious appetite and unquenchable energy, spent her life keeping a succession of three-room apartments aggressively, almost pathologically clean. His youngest aunt had, at birth, been designated by her mother as caretaker, and had not been free to marry until after her mother's death. His own younger sister never outgrew the shackles of her family. He was also astute enough to realize that the fate of women in his family was not uncommon in society at large.

In this light, his unconscious but quite unmistakable decision to raise me as a boy was an act of love. He saved my life, rescuing me from what he must have perceived, even if he couldn't articulate it, as the minefield of girlhood. And how easy, how harmless, to execute this fantasy! In diapers, and later in underpants, I must have looked just like a little boy.

Being raised this way was no burden. It wasn't so much that my femininity was denied—I wore my share of frilly dresses, spring coats with velvet collar trim, and black patent-leather Mary Janes, along with pocketbooks to match—as that my masculinity was allowed to flourish. I was plump and hearty, and I loved to eat. My curly red hair was always cropped short. I coveted my father's tools, his flannel shirts, his ties. And my favorite item of clothing, which alone was salvaged and to this day rests in a box atop my mother's closet, was a pair of dungaree overalls.

Yet I suffered no confusion as a child. "Teach me to throw like a boy," I demanded of my father, implying that I knew I wasn't one. It also seemed clear that a girl who could throw like a boy would enjoy the best of both worlds. Why not both? Who would turn down an offer of two for the price of one—especially since being a woman wasn't, to my eyes, particularly interesting.

Sunday morning. We are going to visit my grandparents in the Bronx, as we do nearly every Sunday. My mother is getting dressed, and I am allowed to watch. She plants her heels on her dresser top, points her toes ballerina style, and unfurls the length of her gathered stocking to encase her calf, knee, and thigh, her fingertips nibbling the flesh like little mice. Then she gets the dress from its hanger, and raising her arms, as if to say Hallelujah, she lets it descend around her, making a soft rustling sound. Next she combs her hair, scraping the comb's edge against her scalp to make a part. Now she upends her perfume bottle, a cloudy green glass vial on a china tray on a doily on her dresser, and with the fleshy part of her finger dabs twice behind each ear. Makeup last—a dash of powder to the cheek, nose, chin, and forehead. Eyebrow pencil. Lipstick, the metallic vial uncapped with one hand, color applied from left to right on top, paying no attention to the heart-shaped indentation on her upper lip, then right to left below. Grinding her lips together, she reaches for a tissue on which to blot them, making a perfect red butterfly.

When she's gone, I walk dreamily into her closet, nestling myself in its midst to feel her clothes against me, to put her shoes on my hands. The red silk shirtwaist dress, the black velvet shoes with their stubby high heels and open toes, whisper to me of another life she led, perhaps still leads. So do the bobby pins she keeps in her top dresser drawer, the ones she uses to curl her hair.

I would have done anything to know how to comb my hair, to smell like her, to have a drawer of silky nightgowns to wear at night instead of the embarrassing cotton pajamas with pants that were both too short and too wide. Longingly I coveted her jewelry box, full of necklaces and pins, and the sturdy sea-green perfume bottle atop her dresser. The only costume I was ever interested in for Halloween was to dress up as an adult woman—hose, high heels, and earrings. I desperately wanted to look like her, to move as she did, to rustle the way she did.

But my father, my tall, dark-haired, mysterious father, who could fix everything and make anything out of nothing, was who I wanted to be.

Supine on the living room floor of our Queens apartment, the carpet a dull green, my arms crossed over my chest, my father riveting my ankles, I take a deep breath. If I can perform thirty sit-ups and twenty push-ups, I'll be allowed to participate in the physical fitness assembly. My sixth-grade teacher, assuming I lacked the requisite strength and endurance, didn't initially select me; I had to beg for an audition.

Halfway through my sit-ups, a flaming pain sears my stomach from one side clear across to the other. I keep going, complete twenty, and turn over. Push-ups are even worse. To lift myself off the floor using the strength in my upper arms feels impossible, gravity a boot bottom flat on my back. "Keep your back straight," my father advises. My arms tingle, tremble, falter. Nose to the carpet, my toes flexed and digging into the floor, I eke out the energy for one more push-up, then one more.

I pass the audition; I'm in the show. What I remember best, however, is my teacher's lack of surprise. "Good," is all she says when I am done. "You're in."

"I'm in," I say to myself over and over, back in my seat, the blood pounding between my ears, sweat drying on my skin. I've accomplished what I wanted to, my will as strong as my biceps.

"Pitch it in here, right here, baby, come on, come on, you can do it, right here, the sweet spot." Sherry and I, best friends since fourth grade, took turns batting and pitching on the local baseball field, mired in early-spring mud. We had only the skinniest window of time in which to practice: between the earliest signs of thaw—sometimes we wore mittens under our fielding gloves—and the onset of Little League season, when hordes of uniformed boys would overrun our favorite fields.

We were perfecting our batting stance, swing, and fastball. Other friends would occasionally join us after school or on Saturday afternoons, but they were in it for a good time; for Sherry and me it was sustenance. Scions of National League families, we nonetheless worshiped the dynastic, unbeatable Yankees. Building character meant nothing to us. We needed victory.

But by the spring of sixth grade, I noticed that I looked forward to our afternoon practice sessions more than Sherry did. The other girls had stopped coming entirely. They'd rather walk down to the recently opened pizzeria, the first in our neighborhood, and wait for a pack of boys to saunter in. Or spend hours in the candy store, picking up one and then another movie magazine. They began wearing bras. Watching Mr. Novak. Dr. Kildare. Ben Casey.

"They're turning into TTAs," was my father's explanation. It stood for Typical Teen Agers, a term he'd coined for those girls who squealed and giggled and paid entirely too much attention to their hair. He said it with a smile, but he was only half amused. Other men's daughters could turn into stereotypes, but not me.

Or so he thought. In fact, even I wasn't immune to their influence. Over time, goaded by my friends, I had distilled my lavish but diffuse love of baseball onto one player, the ace of the Yankee pitching staff, Whitey Ford.

Why Whitey? Well, Sherry had already targeted Mickey Mantle. Bobby Richardson and Tony Kubek were cute but nondescript. Yogi Berra was gnomelike, and too much of a buffoon. Whitey, on the other hand, was quite simply the winningest pitcher on the winningest team. He was reliable. He was reasonably cute, as far as I could tell. And by idolizing him I accomplished several tasks at once.

To the casual observer—to my father—I still looked like Rutherford, my face buried in the sports pages, my eyes glued to the game. Even I was convinced that reading *Sports Illustrated* was nothing like poring through *TV Guide.* My friends who coveted movie magazines were TTAs, but I—combing the Queens library system to find *The Whitey Ford Story,* replete with black-and-white photos of his rookie year, his wife, his kids—was still simply a sports fan, doing my job.

Yet when I needed to reassure my friends—and myself—that Roberta was alive and well, Whitey would come to my emotional rescue. The fact that I loved him, that I was as crush-riddled as they were, proved that I was indeed a girl.

Though not entirely. The more unswerving I remained in my devotion to Whitey, the more I undid myself. My friends weren't up to true love; they weren't interested in fidelity. Back and forth they wavered, unable to make up their minds, endlessly debating who was cuter—Richard Chamberlain one week, Vince Edwards the next. Who could keep up? Worst of all, their limitless inconstancy didn't embarrass but delighted them; it was all part of the game.

The ultimate definition of a TTA was a girl who couldn't make up her mind. What neither my father nor I could stomach was my friends' fickleness. We didn't understand the function it served: that staring at their idols, they were intently trying to discover not merely who was cutest but also who appealed to them—and, ultimately, what it meant to be attracted.

This elusive issue of physical attraction was one I entirely sidestepped, as if I alone had been vaccinated against a catastrophic illness that was striking down all my friends. Pinned to the ground, a knee at my throat, I still couldn't have coughed up my answer to the question "Who's cuter?"—Paul or John, Kildare or Casey. And it wasn't for lack of trying. I'd stare at their faces for hours at a time, but in the end the images would dissolve into a swirling chaos of newsprint dots, much the way repeating a word, any word, soon enough renders it meaningless. Flipping out over a man was as artificial an activity to me as having to hunt for food. The connection from my eye—from all my senses—to the master sexual switch buried somewhere within me had been severed, or not yet forged. "P.S. Watch Beatles—7:00, channel 7." I may have been the only girl in America who needed to give herself such a reminder.

Because I knew my friends were onto something I couldn't even imagine, I subjected them to the same withering scorn my mother reserved for baseball: "Guess I'll watch D.K. tonight," I wrote in my diary one night. "It's absolute crap but there's nothing else on."

With each passing day, baseball became the perfect vehicle for a cross-dresser like me. Whitey Ford was less my idol than my alibi, my foxhole, my much-needed camouflage. As with an uncle who used to place his copy of *Playboy* within the folds of a *Look* magazine so he could read it in the living room while the kids watched television, baseball provided me with much-needed cover. It simultaneously assured my father that I was still Rutherford; needled my mother that I wasn't following in her footsteps; set me apart from my friends, who were plunging into the frightening waters of teenage sexuality while I stood on shore, afraid to wade in; and gave me the opportunity to practice being a typical teenager nursing a crush even though I was only lip-synching. In other words, it enabled me to look to the world like the boy I'd always been while turning slowly into a girl.

Tennis was our first sport in eighth grade. First we received a four-page mimeographed set of rules, on which we were quizzed. Then we watched Mrs. Cooper and Miss Smith hit balls to each other, explaining each missed shot. Finally, we were given tennis rackets and let loose on the court.

Fortunately, my father had taught me to play, translating the skills he'd honed on the handball courts of the Bronx to this more suburban and refined game. The school's courts were on the perimeter of the immense athletic fields, within eye- and earshot of the Long Island Expressway, which whispered of commerce, traffic, and the tantalizing world at large. The weather was cool but not cold, and I loved being outdoors.

I was less enthusiastic about our next sport, field hockey—the ball too small, the field too large, the game too fragmented, the days too cold. Though we were allowed to wear sweatshirts, our legs were bare against the settling chill as the season tunneled toward Halloween, and no one could shake the goose bumps.

By Thanksgiving, the weather forced us indoors, and that's when my trouble began. Dodgeball was a horrible every-girl-for-herself game, the object of which was to hit as many people as you could with a large ball. Denise and I hated it, though for different reasons, she repulsed by the aggression, me by the cattiness of it, the fact that it had more in common with female mud wrestling than with true sport. The incongruous sight of Mrs. Cooper demonstrating the proper technique, holding the ball by her palms, her hands arched to protect her talon-red nails, was too hard to take. Whipping each other up into an idealistic frenzy, we both refused to play.

What I knew about physical activity never found its way into physical education classes but remained *samizdat*—forbidden, subversive, underground. So thoroughly did Miss Smith and Mrs. Cooper wring every ounce of exhilaration from sports, it seemed they must have taken special classes in the technique. Running outdoors, face to the wind, wielding the racket or bat like a bionic arm, exerting muscle against gravity—they shunted all this aside in favor of sitting us in neat rows, drilling us on rules, and forcing us to wear the hated blue uniforms.

Locker room smells that swelled and subsided like the tide, hair clogged in sink drains, the rush to struggle into our clothes before the bell rang (we were supposed to shower, but no one did), jockeying for position at the two mirrors so we could fix our hair before venturing out into the hallway, worrying about how we'd look when we arrived at our next class, skin sweaty and hair stringy—this was junior high school gym.

A *D* in gym on my second report card: I literally didn't believe my eyes. I'd never even gotten a *C*. It must have been a mistake.

Cheeks burning and heart racing, I tore down the halls to confront my tormentor. Mrs. Cooper was smoking, as usual, in her tiny office, staring through the large window at the empty gym, her orangy-tan legs propped up on her desk. For a moment I was distracted by the little pink pom-poms protruding from the back of the terry-cloth socks she wore under her sneakers, and by the smothering scent of pine air-freshener.

I sputtered something; she shrugged, clearly unmoved by how distraught I was. "You earned the grade," she said, exhaling smoke through both nostrils like a dragon. "You had a very poor attitude all semester. And you neglected to lock your locker two times, which is an automatic *D*." Swiveling in her chair, she shrugged and began stuffing cigarettes and papers into her pocketbook.

Retorts ran through my mind: "You'll regret this," "I have friends in high places," "You've tangled with the wrong person." I knew I'd sound ludicrous saying them, but they were true. I'd have the last laugh. I felt powerful, a power memorable not for its novelty but rather for its long history; it was something I'd always felt, though perhaps I was feeling it for the last time.

Abruptly I left and headed like a heat-seeking missile right for Mrs. Eisen's office and vindication. On the way, I ran into Mr. Black. To my two biggest champions I tearfully related the injustice done to me. They were shocked and outraged. "Go home," they told me. It would all be taken care of.

"Dear Mrs. Eisen," my father began, "I signed Roberta's report card, but Mrs. Israeloff and I must protest. We have analyzed the situation in our house all weekend, and could not see our way clear to accept the grade in Physical Education."

I have a copy of this letter, typed on blue onionskin by my mother. Forcefully but not brittlely, my father explained that to his mind the grade was not warranted, and he suggested possible alternative reprisals that would not affect my grade.

> Please confer with Mrs. Cooper on Roberta's behalf to see if she would reconsider and raise the mark to at least a *C*, as this would allow her to be eligible for Honor Society membership.
>
> This is all-important to Roberta. It was a severe blow to her to find out that after all her diligent, concentrated study she was able to maintain her grades in the "major subjects" only to lose out in a "minor" subject.
>
> May I add that Roberta has attached extreme importance to the Honor Society, but we, as her par-

ents, are very proud of her academic showing without official recognition.

I cried the day I discovered this forgotten letter in a shoe box in which I stashed old letters and birthday cards. I'd never known that my father could write with such suppleness. I admired his tone—a balanced blending of conciliation and staunchness, intimacy and touching formality. Stumbling upon physical evidence of the invisible scaffolding he'd painstakingly and invisibly erected for me was like waking from a dream about the beach and finding sand on my pillow.

The letter was mailed on Monday. On Friday, after four days of meetings and conferences, on the phone and in person, my grade was changed to a *B*. I made second honors.

"Come one, girls, move it," Mrs. Cooper cackled, walking through the locker room, reeking of cigarette smoke, hair spray and nail polish.

Winter meant modern dance. No longer did we have to wear hideous blue uniforms; now we had to squeeze, hoist, and jam our sweaty, stubby bodies into black leotards, black tights, and black ballet slippers. My body resisted the form-fitting nylon, which seemed to congeal on my skin after a second's exposure, to undergo a chemical reaction with my pores and refuse to budge. Oh, how I missed the shapeless, lumpish blue uniforms. At least they were equally unbecoming to all of us. In dancers' garb, everyone else looked on her way to womanly and I looked like something whittled from wood—big where I should have been small, flat-chested where I should have been shapely, no curves anywhere, just awkward, jutting angles. Worst of all, I hadn't yet gotten my period, not even a hint, not one false alarm.

On the gym floor we took our places, sitting in neat rows, filling the space like dots on a huge piece of graph paper. When Mrs. Cooper walked in, we were supposed to bend over from our waists, our legs and arms outstretched in a posture of prostration. We waited for the scratch and whine of the tape recorder. Slowly, the tinny, eerie strains of "Stranger in Paradise" blared through the gym, which was always a few degrees cooler than was comfortable. We started to rise to the music, like snakes being charmed. In pink ballet slippers and leotard, Mrs. Cooper patrolled the rows, kicking an out-of-place foot, moving a hip, guiding an arm. The music segued into an upbeat version of "Fly Me to the Moon." This was our cue to rise slowly and turn, our arms swaying side to side.

The routine, choreographed, I suppose, by Mrs. Cooper, went on for a half hour, a medley of different songs with wildly differing tempos and moods, ending with us back on the floor, bent over, moaning slightly to ourselves. "All right, girls, that's it," Mrs. Cooper would yell, stopping the tape, waiting until the echo died down. "Not bad. Not good, but not bad. Don't forget to shower."

She'd turn her back and we'd run for the locker room, dying to stuff ourselves back into our regular clothes, to claim a space in front of the mirror, where we could finally comb our hair. How many more weeks of this torture? I wondered. My body ached; I had a perpetual charley horse. I was too tall to touch my toes, not limber enough to attempt a split. I looked, I was quite sure, about as graceful as a football tackle.

Come spring, as the air warmed and the earth softened, we all longed to be released, to be outdoors in our sweatshirts and bare legs, free to run, to swing a racket, pitch a ball. Even hated field hockey seemed like paradise; at least we could stand in the deep backfield—where the ball never came—for minutes at a time and take deep whiffs of the air, shield our eyes from the sun and watch the mighty river of ceaseless traffic on the Long Island Expressway.

But Mrs. Cooper had other ideas. Amid great fanfare—rolling out an overhead projector, setting up a screen, finding a pointer and an opened box of chalk—she introduced the "Health" portion of our curriculum. We sat clustered on the bleachers as if watching a volleyball game.

Brandishing the pointer as naturally as an extremely long fingernail, Mrs. Cooper indicated the usual diagrams: sweat glands, mammaries, fallopian tubes, ovaries, all in tasteful blues and pinks. She distributed little books, which, for all their charts and maps, somehow managed to obscure as much information as they disseminated. Try as I might, I simply couldn't envision how all those pipes and tubes fit inside me, where exactly they were in relation to recognizable bodily landmarks like belly button and groin, and what I could do to make them work right. Words leapt up from the page into my ears and mind, but pictures sat there, flat and motionless, as inert as my body.

A movie, produced by the makers of a brand of sanitary napkin, didn't help much either. "A wonderful time, a special time," the narrator intoned, every frame infused with a pink glow. If it was so wonderful, why couldn't anyone talk about it head-on? Why all the evasions and euphemisms?

"Don't even think of asking to be excused from gym because you have your period," Mrs. Cooper told us, emerging from her office—to which she'd retreated for a cigarette—smoke streaming out of her nostrils. She rewound the movie, fiddled with the pointer, placing its metal end on the floor, fingering its rubber point. To her, menstruation was neither mystical nor special; it was primarily a logistical and hygienic problem, something that complicated her life, drove her to cigarettes. "And don't think you can get away with using perfume. Perfume doesn't erase sweat. It's still there. You just have to get in the shower. Every day. Especially that time of the month."

Most girls had already been visited by their "friend," as we called it; I didn't know who else besides me had not. My slowness mortified me. I felt frozen in a netherworld that admitted only me: clearly no longer boy, but not girl either. Hormone levels were something I couldn't study for, couldn't influence no matter how hard I tried. I felt like a colossal failure. Worse, I felt upside down. The one thing that came naturally to every other woman in the world came hard for me. I had to be vigilant where everyone else simply sat back and let her juices flow.

"Any questions?" Miss Smith asked. No one budged. I wanted to ask why both versions of womanhood—the movie's soft-music-and-roses rendition and Mrs. Cooper's it's-nothing-but-an-annoyance attitude—were both so unappealing. Neither seemed right, neither made sense. Yet how could I have spoken? I had no authority, I was ignorant, I was delayed, possibly deformed, so I kept my mouth shut. So did everyone else. The teachers shrugged and dismissed us a few minutes before the period was up; I guess the session had exhausted them too.

We tore out of the musty gym like a pack of wolves and took to the halls clamorously, our frenzied energy barely under wraps. Ahead of us was the boys' gym, the door open just a crack. There were Rod and Eddie, all the boys gathered on bleachers as we had been, the coach barking at them, whistle round his neck, pointer in his hand.

Had they seen a movie too? What was the boys' version? What did their diagrams look like? The coach blew a short whistle for quiet, but nothing seemed to stop the low-level snickering, like static on the radio. For the rest of the day, the snickering continued, in the halls and classrooms. Every boy, even the most pimply and shy, was capable of joining in at any moment, claiming all the while that he couldn't help it.

During a softball game in June, I struck out on three swings and then bobbled a ball at second base that should have been an easy out. Someone groaned. When I looked up, I saw a girl from my homeroom rolling her eyes at her friend; they were both staring at me.

It was one of those slow-motion moments, when one finds herself unable to move. I felt as if I'd become a tree rooted to the earth, as if I'd tumbled into a bottomless cavern. I'd humiliated myself. Or rather, I'd just become aware of an entire year's worth of humiliation. Thinking of myself as a boy just wasn't working anymore. And I wasn't doing too well as a girl.

If this had been a movie scene, I would have begun walking through the infield, even as the next ball was pitched, discarding my glove as I walked. I would have dressed slowly and closed my locker in such a way that everyone would know I'd never be back.

My retirement lasted nearly ten years. In college I discovered badminton and became a pretty good player. It's the only competitive sport I can play, and it perfectly embodies my predicament: I bring all my strength to bear, but on something as inconsequential, as nonthreatening, as puny as a shuttlecock. It's the sport for people who are all suited up but have no place to go.

During graduate school, long days filled with nothing but reading and writing, sitting at one desk or another, a colleague of mine suggested that we try running. We met out on the quarter-mile track and jogged around once, twice, three times. Some of our friends joined us. Muscles appeared. The cramp in my side from breathing too heavily went quickly away.

Running was perfect for me: I could do it alone, I didn't have to keep score or try to beat anyone. I especially loved running in winter, when, bundled in sweat clothes and a muffler, I felt like a portable generator, as if the snow surrounding my footfalls on the barely discernible paths in Riverside Park melted on contact.

I ran for several years, until indoor bicycling on a bike that went nowhere became more viable, saving me time. Hitting the wall is still the point of it all—that moment when you feel as if you simply can't go on, then find that by putting your head down and slightly closing your eyes, you've come out on the other side of some gossamer membrane, feeling as if you're immortal, as if you could go on forever.

"Just try it," my younger son, Jake, implores me. He's been practicing dribbling a basketball between his legs for the past three weeks. He shows me how to spin around at the last second. I'm klutzy with the ball. I'd rather shoot some baskets. I try some bank shots and layups, and wonder if he realizes how athletic I am. I've played catch with my sons, I've Rollerbladed, I take them ice- and roller-skating, and never once have they commented on my coordination. I keep wanting to ask them, "Do you realize that I'm good at this stuff? Do you realize that I throw like a boy, not like a girl?"

They don't notice, of course. They don't even notice that they're the ones to break off the game, not me. They like sports, but neither has the passion that I brought to baseball. Creatures of the nineties, they're indoor kids, more interested in virtual basketball than in actually running up and down a court.

It's true, however, that they never see me play competitive sports. In fact, when kids gather on our driveway for a game of three-on-three hoops, or even tackle football in the fall, I hold my breath. I'm afraid of the contact. I see the killer instinct in their eyes, their hunger for victory, and I want to turn away.

Competition scares me, has scared me ever since eighth grade. Questing after absolute victory was a grail I abandoned and to which I never returned. "You have to learn to push yourself," my husband tells me. We're hitting a tennis ball back and forth to each other. He's trying to convince me to take tennis lessons with him. He thinks I'm ready to get competitive, to realize that winning a tennis game won't kill me, and neither will losing.

"Whack it," he yells at me when he senses that I pull back from a shot. "What are you afraid of?" Next time I follow his advice and let loose. The ball goes exactly where I want it to, where he isn't, and the point is mine. I can't stop grinning.

"Okay," I tell him when darkness ends our game. "I'll try lessons." I feel more exhilarated than I have in years, but I know exactly what I'm afraid of: that if I run too fast or far, if I summon every ounce of energy in my body, I'll burst, like a supersonic plane, through the gender barrier and turn once and for all into the boy I was supposed to be.

OCTOBER 13:

Say, who's that coming down the hall? My, but she's tall! And skinny too! Well, not really—*but again, skinnier than most! It looks like she has brown, curly hair streaming down an oval face. Plain brown eyebrows and long eyelashes surround the almond shaped eyes, and accent her features. The color depends on the light; the eyes are brown and sometimes hazel. She has a fair complexion, except when she's excited and her cheeks turn red. Then, of course, she's like everyone else with two ears! Plain, regular ears flat against her head, but then again, ears are ears! Well, well, if it isn't good ole Roberta! Oh, nothing much, we were just saying how perfectly normal you are! So perfectly normal!*

Worse than our first assigned paragraph, to write about a mistake, was the self-portrait Mrs. Johnson had asked us to write. How did she manage to come up with such lousy topics? As a protest, I'd written mine without once consulting a mirror.

Almond-shaped eyes? Fair complexion? These were phrases I'd read in books. I had no idea what they meant, much less if they accurately applied to me. In fact, I had no sense of how I looked. "In one man's opinion" was a phrase I routinely used in my dairy to introduce my own thoughts, as if I hadn't even noticed that I wasn't, in fact, a man.

"Cleverly handled," Mrs. Johnson wrote, referring, I suppose, to my decision to compose a portrait in motion, as if viewing myself walking down a hall. Yet curiously I didn't describe the way I walked, perhaps because my parents had made me self-conscious, informing me that I walked "like a boy."

"However, you are distinctive, not 'normal' or average," Mrs. Johnson continued. "Your hair isn't simply brown but red and gold as well. Why not include your sparkling smile and add color with it? The mood and style of the writing gives the piece a definite lift. *B+*."

Two weeks later, I handed in a rewrite, which differed only slightly:

> It looks like she has brown hair, but wait, red highlights show up as the light hits it. Anyway, this thick bush of unruly hair streams down her oval shaped face. . . . Excitement lights up her whole face; the eyes twinkle, her lips and cheeks become rosy. Frequently, she resorts to her smile, a little thing, but quite rewarding. Then, she's like everyone else, with two ears.
>
> Well, if it isn't good ole Roberta! Gee, I thought it was you. There's something about you only you have. Yup, only you!!

The last paragraph is forced. I wrote it to satisfy Mrs. Johnson, a wholly different activity than wanting to please Mr. Black. He was the one I needed to impress. In English, I was merely trying to do what was expected. Meeting expectations was a reflex with me—a habit so strong I couldn't break it even though I scorned these artificially short papers we were being asked to write, this focusing on what we did wrong and what we looked like. English had always been about the world out there, not the world within. I wasn't yet interested in myself, not as an object of scrutiny: that perspective would take years to evolve, blossoming more than two and a half decades later, after having a baby made me think that something momentous had finally happened to me, something worth thinking and writing about, something others might find value in as well.

Cit. ed., meanwhile, barreled along, Mr. Black dictating notes as if he were trying to determine exactly how fast the car he was madly driving would go. We had tests twice a month now—on the Constitution and the Bill of Rights, on the national court structure, on federal departments and agencies. He also devoted one day a week to current events, an innovative touch that was nonetheless long overdue. The news of the day belonged in school—ever since President Kennedy had been assassinated during school hours, the news landing like a bullet in the middle of math class, stunning us into unnatural silence. Yet Mr. Black didn't confine himself to the upcoming election or the formation of the Warren Commission; we followed England's Parliamentary crisis, changes in the Soviet Communist Party, and Fidel Castro.

All the while, we were compiling the campaign scrapbooks that were due the week before the election. Chronicling the candidates' travels and speeches across the country made the election feel very immediate. We all were rooting for Johnson, of course; everyone knew Goldwater was a dangerous extremist, and anyway, most of our parents were Democrats. Those of us who followed Goldwater had the uphill assignment. It seemed somehow more challenging to attend to a candidate for whom you wouldn't vote.

I entitled my scrapbook "On the Goldwater Bandwagon." Every day, I cut out an article from the *New York Times,* underlined salient passages, and added a brief editorial comment, mostly noting the senator's obsession with communism and calling him to task for his occasional inconsistency. My earliest annotations dripped sarcasm; by the end of the campaign, however, my tone softened. Editorializing less, I simply reported on what he had to say. I'd inadvertently developed a grudging respect for him, the kind that emerges with familiarity. Back and forth across the country he traipsed, sounding his alarmist message in carefully crafted speeches—no televised sound bites in 1964—to crowds gathered in convention halls and factories, schools and train stations, stopping for two days out of respect for former President Herbert Hoover, who died midcampaign. He seemed almost gentlemanly.

But politics—like life, like life in cit. ed.—was rough-and-tumble, and there wasn't too much room for courtly gestures. The winner's circle accommodated only one, as Mr. Black reminded us again and again.

The *A* I received on my campaign journal was entirely anticlimactic, for me and everyone else. Others had comments scrawled in margins, huge question marks, sarcastic notes; mine contained nothing but a grade in a circle on the first page. I was turning into Queen Midas. Everything I wrote for this man turned to gold. And I wasn't sure why.

It's ten o'clock at night; I am in bed, crying. My mother sits next to me. "I can't take this anymore," she says. "You're making yourself crazy. You're putting too much pressure on yourself." She tries to remove my cit. ed. textbook from my hand, but I hold on to it. Tomorrow is a test, and I don't think I'm prepared. If I don't get another 100, I'll get less than 100 in cit. ed., and that won't offset my English and science grades, and as a result I'll receive only second honors.

"If you didn't study at all, if you didn't even open the book, you could get a seventy-five, you could pass."

She means to comfort me, to reassure me, I know, but it's absolutely hopeless; she simply doesn't understand. What would I possibly want with a 75? I rave to myself. A 75 on a social studies test is like breaking a three-day fast with a meal of moldy bread crusts, or being forced to wear a patched and stained hand-me-down dress to Rod's bar mitzvah: in other words, worse than nothing.

"If you can't get ahold of yourself, then I'll have to do something," my mother says. She quite frankly doesn't know what to make of me. I've heard her say on many occasions that she was perfectly happy with the *B*'s and *C*'s she received in college. But her life and mine barely intersect anymore. To her, time is static, repetitious, every day the same routine, week after boring week. What does she know of excellence, of drive, of forward motion? I see my life as a rocket soaring through space in search of brighter and more dazzling rewards, while she circles in sameness, cleaning first the living room and then the bedrooms, one by one, with infuriating regularity and stoicism.

"I'll take you out of track 1," she says slowly and half to herself, surprised to find herself alighting upon so elementary a resolution. "I'm calling Mrs. Eisen tomorrow morning and having her put you in track 2. It's ridiculous to have you up all hours of the night, crying about a test."

But this possibility sends me over the edge. "No," I begin to scream, "you can't do that, don't do that, don't call her, I can't leave my class." Now I'm caught. The more hysterical I become, the more likely she is to follow through; on the other hand, how can I convince her that this is an unthinkable action? I can't leave the class. I just can't.

I sob; she averts her face; we are conversing in different languages. My father walks in. I settle down. He'll translate for me, explain things to her. The light is turned out, even though I want to read the chapter one more time. We don't speak anymore of my being demoted.

FOREIGN LANGUAGE

Strictly speaking, French was my third foreign language. First came Yiddish, then baseball.

"I can't stand those stupid announcers," my mother seethes through clenched teeth. "The same drivel, week after week. They must get paid by the word."

It's a Sunday afternoon—every Sunday afternoon of my childhood—and my family is gathered in the living room of the Bronx apartment of my paternal grandparents. My mother and my grandmother sit together on the couch, talking softly in a seamless mix of English and Yiddish; my father sits in an armchair, occasionally answering questions from his mother; my sister pads from room to room. These are ritualized visits, though we pretend otherwise. In a moment my grandmother, who can't sit still for long, will get up and retrieve from the kitchen a cut-glass bowl laden with Golden Delicious Apples. She'll offer one to each of us, and we'll say no, except for my grandfather, who, in his recliner, will simply shoo her away with his hand.

Seriously overweight, he has to conserve his movements. His enormous belly is roughly spherical, as if he'd swallowed a barrelful of baseballs. Watching him watch a baseball game, I wonder if this isn't the same game he was watching last week, if he's once left his seat since our previous visit.

I am sitting on the floor next to him. We make an interesting team, separated by sex and nearly sixty years. Miraculously, the patriarchal immunity extended to him drapes over my insubstantial shoulders as well. In a family that values consideration, politeness, and formality more than anything, my grandfather and—by dint of sheer proximity—I are granted a weekly exemption. We escape through a gaping loophole, free to be as ill-behaved and ill-bred as I can imagine, excused from the ritualistic questions and answers that pass for conversation, free to squander our attention on something as ridiculous as baseball.

We watch in virtual silence. He is not a natural teacher—he assumes I know more than I do—so I try to absorb as much as I can on my own and ask about only the truly perplexing aspects of the game. He has three cornerstone biases: a pitcher should be allowed to finish his own game; managers interfere too much; batters who step out of the box to spit on their hands and otherwise delay the game are bums.

When I play baseball with my friends in the neighborhood, it's an activity; here, in my grandparents' living room, it becomes a language—of achievement, of competition—whose intricacies I can plumb simply by watching. To the uneducated eye, baseball is a game in which little happens. But the cognoscenti know that each at-bat and pitch is vital, that every pause is fraught with meaning and potential, that the winning run culminates from a host of nearly microscopic events. And someone—an announcer confiding to a live mike, a scout sipping a beer in the stands—is always not only watching and noticing but remembering.

My family communicated in a similar way. The more essential the message, the more deeply buried, and the more urgent that it remain so. To me, as the first child of a Jewish family only two generations out of the shtetl, the commandment to do well in school was never spoken aloud. It didn't need to be. By kindergarten I already knew enough to feel terrible that I wasn't Maxine Klingsbrun, the girl who could read the *New York Times* while our teacher beamed, as if she were personally responsible.

From baseball—from my father—I knew that scores were being kept by somebody, somewhere, even if we weren't aware of it. No statistic was too arcane. "Who cares what he batted during his last year of triple-A ball?" my mother would ask, throwing up her hands in exasperation.

But her question was disingenuous—and she knew it. *Everything* mattered. Successful students had to keep track not merely of report card grades and test scores but of the thousands of ways in which evaluation was doled out: every called-out answer, every casual check or minus dealt out on a homework assignment, every equation solved on the blackboard, and all the throwaway comments, such as "Good story" or "Nice try."

That's why I approached school each day the way a batter tending his average approaches the plate, fully expecting to beat out the bunt, to stretch a single into a double, to cause a stir, generate talk, create notice. Watching games with my grandfather week after week gave me a template with which to evaluate performance. On deck, at bat, on the bench, on the mound, in the field—baseball players became my tutors in competition. How did Whitey Ford *bear* it? I asked myself over and over after the 1963 series, in which he was dealt two stunning personal defeats by Sandy Koufax, the Yankees routed four games to none—how did he or any of his proud teammates have the courage to walk off the field, to talk to reporters, to go home and face their families and friends and last the long winter? What did you do when you wanted to win so much and were handed a plateful of defeat? I read the sports page every day, looking for answers.

If baseball was the language of performance, which the men spoke and the women pretended not to understand, then Yiddish, spoken by women and ignored by men, was the language of inaction—the language of secrets, of *tsouris,* of heartache and betrayal, the language of last resort. There was nothing delicate or subtle about it. It was also the language of ambush. In my mother's or my grandmother's mouth, any ordinary English sentence could at any moment veer off into the guttural, throat-clogging sounds of Yiddish and back again, without so much as a breath-catch. Everything pertaining to the body—passing gas, burping, having sex, needing a tissue—was reserved for indelicate Yiddish, usually accompanied by coarse laughter and a world-weary "Darling-I've-seen-it-all" sadness around the eyes. I was an adult studying German in college before I realized that my mother's mother spoke virtually no English at all.

"Speak English," my sister and I would whine when they forgot to switch back and we found ourselves hopelessly lost. In fact, we understood plenty: from the names we heard, we were able to piece together a pretty accurate sense of what was what—that my aunt's marriage was on the rocks, that the man downstairs liked to wear his wife's underwear, that a second cousin's husband lost his job, *nebech,* what a pathetic loser he turned out to be.

What I didn't realize at the time was that Yiddish was their native tongue, their *mammaloschen,* that they'd never learned to translate their innermost feelings into English. To my grandmothers, certainly, and even to my mother, English was a second language, the language of the stranger, of the host welcoming guests, the language of formality and expectation, of small talk and decorum. All that was transcendently true belonged in Yiddish, and every truth became a secret hidden away in the folds of a language so spirited it spritzed, chortled, and chuckled even in its death throes.

But at a certain point, they even ran out of Yiddish.

Simply put, my family distrusted language. Words were a trap: you could say too much and dig yourself into a hole from which you'd never be rescued; you could inadvertently say what you didn't mean; others could twist and misconstrue what you said, and you'd never have a chance to set it right. People who talked too much suffered from the same scathing opprobrium as those who kept a sloppy house or overate. Best to leave the important things unsaid, packed between the lines.

Or to say, "Oke," as my grandfather did, short for "Okay," his standard response to comments ranging from "Hello" to "Do you take your coffee with milk?" to "How's business?" Like baseball players who minced their words and looked as if their shoes pinched every time they came face-to-face with a microphone, my entire family was short with speech, the volume of what went unsaid far outweighing what we allowed ourselves to utter.

Initially I admired this refusal to speak, to elaborate. But I began to notice, as my grandfather and I continued to watch games together, as Whitey Ford and his aging arm had to fight for a spot on the rotation, that taciturnity was at odds with baseball's inherent, incorrigible sociability: the countless conferences on the mound, the inevitable pause between pitches, the enormous weight of precedent for nearly every play, the endless amount of talk a squib hit or a backhand toss could generate.

Soon I was paying less attention to the close-lipped players than to the announcers, those loquacious men paid to talk more than any woman, to kill time while the players spat and paced, crossed, pinched, and poked themselves. They were devotees of talk for talk's sake—a concept of language wholly foreign to me. Not caring whether they were accurate or honest, they were free to associate, almost wildly, to say whatever came into their heads. They held nothing back. They didn't think before they spoke, they simply emptied the trash bins of their heads into the patient microphone. Quite simply, I fell in love with the idea that there was always something to say.

Mme. Rizzoli was as garrulous as any baseball announcer. Her pedagogic method was to open the floodgates and let French wash over us until we were forced to gasp for air.

Most of my classmates were entering their second year of foreign language; luckily for me, I'd studied it for twice as long. In fourth grade, my class had been selected to participate in an inspired pilot program, long since abandoned. For an hour each afternoon, Mme. Vitel, a native teacher from Gabon, came into our room, pointed at the door, and announced, *"La porte!"* as if delighted by the discovery. Her cheekbones were high and prominent, lips dusky rose and pliable, jaw loose and powerful; we couldn't wait to contort faces and try to re-create the luxuriant, exotic sounds that came out of her mouth.

Within weeks, we'd learned to tell time, to name the features of our faces and all the parts of our bodies, to sing French songs, and to stage a play, "The Strange Case of Little Red Riding Hood and Her Brother," entirely in French.

French lessons with Mme. Vitel continued through sixth grade. When we had to choose a foreign language for junior high, I insisted on French, though everyone else advised the practicality of Spanish. Too late for me; I'd already fallen in love with Mme. Vitel's native tongue. Thanks to her teaching, I didn't have to study French for one second in seventh grade.

By eighth grade, however, my dream of mastering French began to slip out of reach. "Français, the language of tact, of diplomacy, of romance," Mme. Rizzoli cooed, but to those of us trying to memorize irregular verbs and the subjunctive, terms we couldn't even define in English, French remained a recalcitrant block of subject matter at which we had to chip away monotonously, a noun at a time. The prospect of ever saying anything intimate, anything meaningful, seemed increasingly remote. Worst of all, my accent, which had always struck me as *tres charmant,* made Mme. Rizzoli wince ever so slightly.

My language problems extended beyond French, unfortunately, into my social relationships. In elementary school, I'd spoken a dialect of baseball with all my girlfriends: our friendships were predicated either on activity, whether playing ball or riding bikes, or on academic achievement. Alice and Beth, however, were curiously sedentary. Though I rode my bike to their houses, they were driven by their moms to mine; at the community pool where we spent the summer, they cared less about swimming than about applying suntan oil and sunbathing.

Their inactivity made my bike riding and pickup touch-football games with the boys on my block seem juvenile, even perverse. I wanted their approval; more, I wanted to be like them. They were growing up. If I kept pace with them, maybe I could outrun the bad case of arrested development that was stalking me.

"Call me tonight," Alice said casually as we were leaving school one day—a thrilling invitation. After dinner I dialed her number. She had her own pink princess phone, which sat on her desk but could reach to her bed, where she sat cross-legged, leaning against her pillows; I was tethered to the wall phone in the kitchen, the cord only long enough for me to find refuge in a corner of the adjacent dining room. I turned my back to my family, lowered my voice—if only we'd had our own version of Yiddish to speak to each other—and stayed on the phone for well over an hour.

"Alice is such a great kid," I wrote in my diary. "I can talk to her about anything."

"You saw each other in school all day; what do you still have to say to each other?" my mother would ask me, both accusatory and curious. True to our family's linguistic tradition, her more trenchant question hung unspoken in the air between us: "And how come you never talk to me?"

Quite simply, my girlfriends and I couldn't get enough of each other. Our web of friendship had sprung up in English, that deathly subject. Gravitating toward one another, Beth, Alice, Denise, and I formed a coven in the center seats, communicating by sighing deeply to signify our boredom, rolling our eyes, kicking each other's chairs, and circulating an endless stream of notes—a network that didn't end when English was over, or even when school was dismissed. Afternoons, I'd find myself sitting on Alice's bed, or Beth's, pondering life, boys, Mr. Black. Separated for dinner, we picked up the phone to continue talking.

Evening phone calls took on the solemnity of ritual: first you called whoever happened to be your best friend that week, then you moved on down the list in hierarchical order, ending up by speaking yet again to your best friend, to hash over what you'd talked about with everyone else. Often I could tell, by the sequence of busy signals, exactly who was on the phone with whom. And when our parents yelled at us to get off the phone and finish our homework, we wrote notes to each other—long, typewritten notes that we folded into taut, flat little squares to hand out, like candy, the next morning in homeroom. Like members of an underground press that flourished despite being outlawed by a repressive regime, we generated volumes of words each day meant for one another's eyes only.

The notes, many of which I saved and which I now reread, are about nothing at all except the paramount importance of staying in touch. Within this cocoon of language I felt welcomed, safe, and valued—and finally fluent. My friends and I concocted a language with which to express intimate connection and secrets, the physical and the philosophical, a perfect marriage of Yiddish, baseball, and French. We clothed ourselves in our conversation; every book we read, every poem we wrote, every transient feeling and mood, we tried on for each other and modeled as if in front of a mirror: Look at me! Please like me, accept me. I'm really just like you. . . .

But of course, we kept secrets from each other, we talked behind each other's backs, we betrayed confidences on a daily basis. In a conversation with Alice, for instance, I could talk about the look Rod had given Denise at her locker that afternoon, but I couldn't tell Beth, since she was nursing a crush on Rod that week, or because she was having a fight with Denise. Or I could try to keep it a secret, but then I ran the risk of having Denise tell Beth even though she swore not to, and then I'd have to ad-lib a rationale that assuaged Beth while protecting Denise, and sound convincing to boot.

Truthfulness? This remained the ultimate foreign language. All of us knew that words could wound—that my mother could never tell her mother-in-law how tedious she found the weekly Sunday visits, or how much she resented having to signal our return home by dialing my grandmother's number and letting it ring twice; that I could never tell Beth I didn't like the book she'd just lent me as much as she did. Revealing one's innermost thoughts almost always led to controversy and disagreement. The awareness that what I *really thought* could turn people against me shut me up as thoroughly as a vow of silence.

I cultivated writing because words on the page had less capacity to wound than those offered in conversation. At my desk, I could knead hard, hurtful feelings until they were softer, safer, more acceptable. And those sentences that couldn't be softened or neutered I didn't write—sometimes still don't. But I'm learning to.

I'm lying in bed late one Saturday afternoon. My parents are in the living room, my sister's in her bedroom. The book I'm reading is sad, about a doomed love affair. It makes me wonder about my future—if anyone will want me, truly desire me, not just my mind but my body, though I can't imagine what this means.

My father stirs. I hear him walking down the hall to the bedrooms. He's going to knock at my door, notice that I'm reading, walk toward me. I won't want him to see that I'm on the verge of tears, that the book has affected me so. He'll sit down, make a little joke, and I'll laugh, even though I've heard all his jokes a thousand times. He'll ask me to go downstairs with him. He usually retreats to his workroom around this time on Saturdays, as my mother readies our dinner. I don't really want to go, but it's so hard for me to say no to him. I feel torn. I wish I could somehow tell him how much more I enjoy reading than holding his ruler or marking dimensions with a pencil. There are things I wish I could talk to him about, things I wish he would tell me, but words evaporate as quickly as I think of them. I don't want to talk through another medium anymore. Speaking baseball to my grandfather and carpentry to my father leave the words too mangled, meanings too attenuated. I want to speak directly, from the heart. How can I say that without wounding him?

I busy myself in a new chapter, even though I'm not really reading now, just waiting for him to appear.

But he doesn't. He stops at my sister's room. "Come on," he says. "I'm going downstairs, and I need some help."

She scampers up and eagerly follows him. I feel bereft; the tears I've been choking back, induced by the book, overflow. I feel positively abandoned, repudiated, betrayed, forgotten. It probably isn't the first time he's asked my sister's help rather than mine, but it is a single moment of tremendous clarity: He doesn't want to speak to me. Rutherford's gone: Roberta's alone.

Banished from the basement; in self-exile from the kitchen, where my mother is setting the table, slicing tomatoes. I won't go help her until she asks me to, not a second before. There's no place I belong, no place I fit; no one in my family speaks my language. Worse, when I try to speak, it's an act of betrayal.

I married a loquacious man (of all the prenuptial advice I've ever heard, "Marry for conversation—it's the only thing that lasts," remains the wisest), and my sons have inherited the talkative gene. "I'm in awe of you," I recently told Ben on the way home one afternoon as he told us about Lisa, the cashier he'd just met at the video store: she went to college in Rhode Island, she hoped to become an artist, she was working for the summer and living at home. . . . "You can have a conversation with anyone." Even better, he never doubts that he has something interesting to say.

"It's easy," he said, with the nonchalance of someone who's never spent a tongue-tied minute. "Just begin anywhere." I feel like an insomniac who's advised to close her eyes and relax. But inwardly I'm delighted that what I worked so hard to learn comes naturally to my sons and my husband.

Words don't scare them, and living in their midst has had a salubrious effect on me. I've loosened up, in conversation and on paper. Yet I remain, at heart, a foreign-language student, and as Mme. Rizzoli advised, I have to practice every day. "Recite the dialogues and vocabulary words standing in front of a mirror," she suggested, pacing back and forth, her brightly colored skirt rustling. "Look at your lips, your jaw. *Listen* to yourself."

I'm trying—to overcome my fear of words, to fall in love with truthfulness, to worry less about how others will react to what I have to say, and simply to combine the easy garrulousness of Mme. Rizzoli and Mel Allen with the conviction I bring to conversations with my closest friends.

"I tried to call you last night, but your line was busy," my mother remarks, still a little incredulous, a little jealous. "You must have been talking to Alice."

I was. It's my homework. Without daily practice, I'd

backslide and forget that putting thoughts and feelings into words isn't the same as acting on them; that in fact you can think just about anything and say more than anyone in my family ever dreamed.

NOVEMBER 4:

I only made 2nd honors this time, not first. Tough, I don't really care. Johnson won. Keating didn't. But I don't feel too bad. Man did the Democrats ever have themselves a sweep! End of tests. Thank God.

Politics and current events had no place in English. In an act of pure spite, Mrs. Johnson led us, like a deranged general, on a resolutely backward journey, out of our lively, engaging times and into the dim and dusty past—eighteenth-century Boston and the nineteenth-century Great Plains. To her credit, she didn't dwell on plot—she knew that we despaired of having anything adventurous happen to us—but focused instead almost exclusively on character.

Of course, none of the books we read featured a woman hero. On the contrary, *Johnny Tremain* depicted two female stereotypes—one proud and vain, the other self-sacrificing. Per Hansa, the eponymous giant in the earth, was saddled with Beret, a wife riddled with fear and illness, who embodied the antithesis of the pioneer spirit. Even the book I selected on my own, A. J. Cronin's *The Citadel,* portrayed a martyred wife whose moment of glory arrives when her husband begs her forgiveness.

These women, these pathetic excuses for characters, had nothing to say to me. Reflexively, my girlfriends and I identified with male heroes, men questing to fulfill their destiny, whether Norwegian emigrants struggling to outlast a winter on the Great Plains, or Boston shopkeepers wrestling with their conscience. "Per Hansas all over the world are able to combat and accept evil while rejoicing over the good," I wrote in my book report about *Giants in the Earth*. "Berets dig a hole and crawl in, unable to cope with any undesirable circumstance. This world is full of too many Berets and not enough Pers."

The only strong woman I came across, ironically enough, was Jessie Frémont, the "Immortal Wife" of Irving Stone's historical novel. Jessie, who complains in the book's opening pages that her father, Senator Thomas Benton, wanted her to have been a son, in charge of expeditions to the western frontier, ends up marrying the promising Lieutenant John Frémont. When he chooses not to run for the presidency—a race a character in the book assumes he would have won—because of his antislavery feelings, Jessie's hopes to be First Lady are dashed. My report concludes:

> I only hope my marriage will be the same as the Fremonts. It now seems like even a more wonderful and beautiful thing. Please God don't deprive me of this feeling and beauty in my life. I live for this moment. How I envy Jessie what a great woman she was. I hope my love for whoever I marry will be as true and strong and long lasting. A good marriage is made in Heaven.

"You have to read this book," I told Beth. "It's the best." She took it gladly, hungrily, and gave one to me, the one Alice had just finished, which Denise had recommended. We inhaled one another's favorite books, staying up late at night, reading while walking to school. Then we wrote notes to each other describing—reliving—our favorite parts. Mrs. Johnson's total lack of charisma freed us to turn from the front of the room to each other.

DECEMBER 10:

I am becoming a nervous wreck. I am crying. Honor society isn't worth anything. But if I don't make it, I'll fail my goal. It's more important that I am an individual. But I'm beginning to doubt it! Damn!

English was dragging me down. I wasn't doing well on a type of assignment Mrs. Johnson called "writing design"—a mimeographed narrative truncated midway, for which we had to supply our own ending. Alice, Beth, Denise, and I thought this assignment terribly beneath us. We didn't want to finish anyone else's story any more than we wanted to have someone dress us.

In reality, I hadn't a clue as to how to compose a plot. The endings I constructed were contrived and implausible—a scared-out-of-her-wits baby-sitter who nonetheless falls asleep before discovering the source of the spooky noise outside, for example. This was the first time my writing facility deserted me. I found myself unable to answer the simple question "What happens next?"—a difficulty that persists to this day, thwarting my attempts at fiction writing. Compose a plot, set it in motion? It feels much too presumptuous. Safer to describe events I had no hand in orchestrating, to analyze, probe, perhaps embellish. That way, if challenged, I can offer a simple defense: "But that's what really happened."

Even in Mrs. Johnson's class, my fiction was thinly veiled autobiography—witness the first short story I wrote, cast as a diary entry. "Even Up Here" was about a girl who confronts racism not only in her community but in her own family. The subject had haunted me ever since I'd learned by letter that Mr. Loehman had relocated to North Carolina. "What makes you think racism knows geographical boundaries?" he wrote back to me after I'd expressed shock that he'd chosen to live in the unenlightened South. If anything, he argued, race relations were in many ways easier in his new home; people were less hypocritical. And sure enough, a week or so later I saw an article in the local newspaper about a cross-burning on the lawn of a black family's home just one town away.

Before collecting our stories, Mrs. Johnson asked us to exchange them with our neighbor, and then with another neighbor, for their critiques—a thoroughly shocking request. We had never before been asked to comment on each other's work. Writing for a classmate was entirely different than writing for a teacher. Those sitting next to me weren't authorities; they could say anything. What would their words be worth?

My story went first to a girl from my homeroom, whom I didn't know well. She praised it lavishly. Then she passed it to Beth.

"Verisimilitude was strongest point," Beth wrote. "Characterization wasn't very deep but it didn't detract from the story. It left me wondering what I would do in the same situation."

Mrs. Johnson put tiny red checks in the margin next to Beth's two comments, indicating her agreement. My characters shallow? Didn't that mean I was shallow? How come Beth knew that and I didn't?

DECEMBER 15:

They are ruining me. I've never been so tired. I just don't give a damn about anything any more. Please excuse me tonight.

Of course, I meant exactly the opposite of what I wrote—I gave a damn about everything, more than I ever did in my life, and didn't know what to do about it.

More precisely, the skin that had so commodiously accommodated both Roberta and Rutherford was beginning to chafe. Like a puppetmaster, Mr. Black was pulling strings to unimagined tautness, consolidating his power, letting us know that the work we'd done these past months was nothing more than a warm-up, a few slow laps around the track. The more I achieved in his class, the more he challenged me. And the more isolated I felt. Classmates, even my friends, weren't meeting my eyes. Alone at the pinnacle of success in his class, I had nothing to gain and everything to lose with each passing day. And the newest assignment on the horizon, something he called a "reaction paper," was the worst one yet. Forget essay tests and campaign journals; this project would be the supreme test of our skill in ways we couldn't even imagine. "Ask my former students about it," he taunted us again. He knew we talked about him.

In English, Mrs. Johnson was on the verge of vanishing. If fellow students could critique our work, why did we need her? Her authority had dissipated to the point of vaporization. I needed only Alice, Beth, and Denise to read with, write to.

"Your first oral book reports will be due in January," she told us, rummaging through her purse for something, her mind always elsewhere. In other words, we had to read a book and talk about it. Big deal.

Still, I had to find the right book. What would Alice and Beth choose? I spent hours in the town's dingy storefront library, perusing the shelves, determined to find a book as large as life, to flex my muscles over something that mattered, to rebuke that miniaturist Mrs. Johnson, whose selection of slim volumes spoke loudly of her reluctance to trust us with Real Literature.

Moby Dick was quite simply the biggest classic I could find. I could almost taste Mrs. Johnson's chagrin when she learned of my choice. But this wasn't the book's only allure. It was also a gesture toward my father. Since I'd stopped asking him for help with math and science in all but the most dire circumstances, a gap had opened between us, which neither of us knew how to fill. Reading Melville's masterpiece about the sea while he sat reading the newspaper allowed me to feel connected to him without having to speak or ask him anything.

He loved the sea; we both did. He'd been a sailor during World War II. That he'd left his tight-knit family to train at Cornell and Boston, that his ship passed through the Panama Canal en route to California—all this intrigued me.

He rarely spoke of his navy days. Gradually its traces fell away: he dropped out of touch with his buddy; his uniforms, both winter blues and summer whites, settled at the bottom of his mother's cedar chest. But he still wore his pea jacket when we played catch in the fall. Together we rooted for Navy in its annual football game against Army. And when we went to the beach, his favorite vacation spot, he always looked wistfully out to sea before diving in. He was our family's only swimmer, and when he swam through the choppy surf, his head down for an impossibly long interval, we thought he was never coming up for air.

Willingly, he served as our emissary to the world at large. We sent him out each morning, and at precisely six in the evening he'd return, duck into the kitchen to kiss my mother hello, and retreat to his bedroom. There he stood in front of his dresser as at an altar—I'd peek sometimes, escaping for a few moments from *Superman,* which my sister and I watched on the couch while my mother prepared supper. Like a spy, I'd watch as he emptied his pockets of change, wallet, and keys, folded his papers in his meticulous way, and put everything in its place in his top drawer. Then he'd take off and fold his work pants and hang up his shirt, easing out of one skin into another, the worn dungarees and flannel shirt he wore around the house, as if he were being debriefed. Next stop was the bathroom, where he washed his sturdy hands and stubby fingers deliberately, and dried them digit by digit. Then, thoroughly my father, he was ready to join us for dinner.

But he could never completely wash away his air of mystery. My mother spoke on the phone to friends, wrote to her old boss, and kept a hat with a feather and veil on the top shelf of her closet. There were things I didn't know about her, but she lived, I was quite sure, only one life. My father sustained an entirely separate identity. He was present and absent, and nowhere was this more evident than when we sat in the living room together, not talking, each of us reading. With *Moby Dick* on my lap, I felt on a par with him.

WINTER

JANUARY 12:

"Call me Ishmael." I'm no one in particular. I could be you, or even me. But call me Ishmael for convenience's sake. I'd like you to come on a voyage with me. Don't ask me why. Somehow, every few years, that invisible police officer of the fates who influences me in every way calls upon me to leave, and see the world. This time, I think I'll embark on a whaling voyage. Come with me. As you'll later see, we're not really embarking on just a voyage to catch whales, but rather one that encompasses all humanity. This was Herman Melville's only purpose in writing his famed epic, Moby Dick.

A white blouse with embroidery along the collar and a brown-and-white pleated skirt—that's what I wore the day I delivered my oral report on *Moby Dick*. Mrs. Johnson and I traded places: I stood behind her desk, she squeezed into my seat, her red pen at the ready. I glanced at my notes, four and a half pages of dense, handwritten script, took a deep breath, and began. Halfway through, I realized to my amazement that without meaning to, I'd memorized it.

My presentation culminated a solid month of work. Night after night during winter vacation, I'd sat in the living room, the heavy book in my hands, determined to read every last word. I didn't take any notes, though I kept a dictionary at hand, and I didn't skip any chapters, even those full of whaling and geographical minutiae that eluded me completely. Intuitively, I understood that the book was an allegory—that the *Pequod* was a microscopic world and its crew humanity, and that the call to voyage is really our journey through life. Best of all, I was beginning to understand that the act of reading was like using a magnifying glass to focus the diffuse rays of the sun: First you lavished all your energies on the narrative, and then it radiated energy back to you.

The evening I finished the book, I began writing my report on a pad of paper from my father's shop. I recently found the draft within my files and was surprised to see how little I'd reworked my words. Only a few sentences were scratched out and recast. Evidently, I'd caught the train of my thoughts and stayed on board—no hesitant stops, no second-guessing, no dead ends.

"And God created great whales": I'd decided to end the report with a line from Genesis. Done—finally. Shuffling the papers, I took a deep breath to steady my quivering legs. How long had I been speaking? I checked the wall clock and finally looked at my audience. No one would meet my eyes. Rod sat as if in a trance, his head at a slight angle, eyes closed. The room was perfectly silent.

I began to panic. Something similar had happened once during seventh-grade English in Queens, a class taught by the exotic Mrs. Araq—a red-haired Jewish woman who had married an Arab and given her daughters lovely Arabic names. I was a little in love with her. One blustery November Thursday, after teaching a lesson about ballads, she asked us to write one. She called on me last, which angered me. When I finished reading, no one spoke. I remember staring out the window at the rain pelting the courtyard, where a few scraggly leaves were trapped, our building a red fortress on the shore of the Long Island Expressway.

Mrs. Araq had never before been at a loss for words. She loved to talk to us, about her daughters, about her husband's work with the U.N., and to read aloud—she had a reedy yet melodious voice—holding books rapturously to her bosom, her nostrils flaring. Certain that I'd erred in some enormous way, I sat down and shoved the paper with my ballad into my desk. Finally, she said, "That was lovely." But she wasn't smiling. She stared at me, as if I'd done something surprising. And I began to realize that the tribute of silence went beyond the power of any grade.

Now silence again, silence that stretched into minutes. Had I miscalculated? Had no one understood? I scanned my friends' faces; they looked away. I was near tears, and my legs felt suddenly weak. Where had I gone wrong?

Mrs. Johnson put her red marking pen in the groove of the desk and began applauding. Suddenly everyone was clapping, and I felt my cheeks flush. One by one, my friends and classmates told me what a good job I'd done. They were impressed, I could tell, not merely by what I'd said but also by how I'd delivered the report. By *me.*

Shakily I took my seat, as the next person walked to the makeshift podium. Mrs. Johnson handed me the sheet on which I'd been graded. There were nine categories of evaluation, ranging from "stance" and "eye contact" to "content" and "pronunciation." I received an Excellent in each, my overall grade an *A+*. Prophetically, Mrs. Johnson wrote: "An excellently planned speech, delivered beautifully. All the deep probing was worthwhile. You will always remember this experience; we will always remember what you shared with us."

I was in a trance, having undergone a sea change as profound as the one about which Melville wrote. I hadn't simply fulfilled an assignment or met an expectation set by someone else. I'd broken through some kind of barrier—I could feel it.

Instead of merely reading about a journey, I'd undertaken one, propelled by an inward desire that originated in the quest for grades and recognition but ended somewhere else entirely. The sheer ambition and scope of the book held me in thrall. The way it spoke beyond itself, to the Bible and other books, it implied an allusive network of literary references that silently communicated with each other as we went about our lives, waiting like patient long-lost siblings to get in touch, a humming community as real as the one binding me to Beth, Alice, and Denise.

For slowly these three girlfriends and I were noticing that our own thoughts had the power to engage us, and to attract others to us. Of course, we'd always been aware of ourselves as thinking, but this was different. The more aware we became of our physical selves—realizing that "cute" in the *Seventeen* magazine sense would never apply to us, that the path to fortune, fame, and popularity wasn't through our looks—the more our self-consciousness became our salvation. We weren't only how we dressed or who we hung out with; we were also the books we read, the dreams we had, the aspirations we shared.

"To be writers!" I'd recently written in an assigned book report posing as a letter to Beth. "This is our quest!" As authors, we would take our place in the great chain of being; via this sacred vocation, we hoped to return, in some small part, the priceless, thrilling gift we were given each time we found, out of all the countless titles in the library, a book we loved.

Our inner lives were what we were discovering, what began slowly to coalesce out of nothingness, the way boys did at parties, always there but never before acknowledged. "Question everything," Mr. Loehman had advised. This year, our little coven began to share our multiplying questions with each other.

My *Moby Dick* report had been my best contribution to our shared endeavor to date. I'd gone beyond simply impressing Mrs. Johnson and my classmates; I'd genuinely moved them. Even boys who'd never before spoken to me muttered compliments in passing. I didn't feel threatening or freakish, which was somehow how I felt after each triumph in Mr. Black's class. In cit. ed. I felt put on display, my talents appropriated, as if I weren't working only for my own benefit but was proving a point on someone else's behalf.

In English that morning there had been no performance and no klieg lights, only a clutch of papers and a desire to explain how this huge and peculiar book, as simple as a fairy tale and impossibly abstruse, had somehow crawled inside me, how it opened me up and made me feel excited, eager, deserving. For the first time all year, English stayed in my mind after the bell rang and I went off to science.

SCIENCE

Miss Delray herself seemed like some kind of scientific experiment—the shrunken woman, the world's most compact and robotic teacher—embodying the imponderable quality I'd come to associate with the subject itself. On the same order of difficulty as why the dinosaurs became extinct was this question, which I posed to my diary early in October: "Why ain't Miss Delray married? So nice . . ."

Clearly, her singular status posed a serious threat to me. I had had unmarried women teachers in the past, but they all were young and simply marking time until the spring morning when they'd waltz into class with their fingers splayed, sparkling diamond positioned on ring finger. Then they would finish the semester and disappear into wedded anonymity.

Miss Delray was clearly older than these other women and didn't seem to be waiting for anything. She'd either already been rejected or done the rejecting herself, a possibility I acknowledged but couldn't swallow. Women weren't in a position to reject—this much I'd absorbed from sheer observation. They were supposed to be welcoming, to accept.

Yet Miss Delray exuded an air of closemouthed self-containment that both thrilled and mystified me. Though I'd never before encountered her combination of traits in a science teacher, I was more than willing to give her a chance. Science and I were old friends, and I well knew that the field was nothing if not gloriously inclusive. Equal parts philosophy, theory, alchemy, technology, and speculation, it was the subject that engaged me as no other. I loved its immense scope and revelatory depths; its messiness and explosiveness; its ability to encompass both past and future.

"Sometime later this year," Miss Delray promised with uncharacteristic vagueness, "we'll dissect a sheep's eye." All the girls groaned; the boys smirked and averted their eyes. Who determined that biology was the arm of science best suited for children steaming in their own hormonal juices? Physics, the study of matter and motion, of the forces of attraction and repulsion, seems much more appropriate. Biology—eggs and sperm, quivering, bloody life—was the very culture in which we swam, and it threatened to engulf us.

But I couldn't be too picky. I'd waited for years to find myself studying a version of science into which I could sink my teeth. Bring on the sheeps' eyes. I couldn't wait.

What does it mean that water seeks its own level? How did they split the atom? Why can't we see an atom? What is a light-year? These are the questions I'd ask my father, most often on those happy occasions when we were alone in the car, a game of intellectual catch, me lobbing questions at him, he fielding them and gently returning answers. Never mind that his explanations usually spun just out of my reach; I loved sitting on the front seat next to him, in my mother's seat, watching telephone poles and mile markers blur by, listening to him.

My father's car was at once safe and exciting, familiar and thrilling, domestic and mystical. We both loved the moment of ignition, when the engine shuddered to life, power rippling through the metal skeleton to the tires, seats, and steering wheel, which jiggered on its mount like life itself. Yet the car was also a miniature house on wheels. Packed into the trunk was everything you'd ever need in an emergency—blankets, flares, spare-tire tools, and jugs of water. It was the kind of car you could safely take on a safari and not worry, though my father drove only to work, and on weekends to the Bronx to visit his parents. In his glove compartment were maps and tire gauges, pencils and napkins, and a little gadget I especially loved, shaped like a stopwatch with a pizza-cutting wheel on the bottom, which, when rolled along a route on a map, told you how many miles you'd have to travel to get from here to there.

"How does that work?" I'd ask him. Teaching didn't come naturally to him. He distrusted words. Thoroughly kinesthetic, he was happiest with something in his hands, to make or fix.

• • •

"Now, the secret to good painting," my father instructs me, "is to not get too much paint on the brush. Dip your brush into the can only about a quarter inch, or half an inch at most." We are sitting together at a card table in the living room, newspaper below us. We are both wearing aprons and old clothes. On the table is a two-step stool my father has built for me so I can reach the bathroom sink. The back is hinged, a thin wood door opening into an oddly shaped storage space, big enough to hold shoe-polishing equipment.

I've been waiting for hours for this moment. We had to assemble the brushes first, then decide which ones were appropriate, clean them, dry them, put the others away. If we don't hurry up, my sister will awaken and it will be time for supper and we won't have finished. But my father will not be rushed. He has a plan.

I try to follow his directions. I understand that he is conferring great dignity on this activity by not doctoring the curriculum to accommodate me. My father and I are the only ones talking. We are the only part of the house that is alive.

I try to follow his instructions. His brush is wide and stubby, like his fingernails; mine is thin. I try to dip the brush into the paint as delicately as he does and to wipe it first this way, then that, on the rim to measure out the right amount, so that when we put the bristles to wood, the brush glides. But either my brush comes up too dry, and I make wispy strokes, or I leave too much on, and the paint clumps in a thick blob. And meanwhile the paint is traveling from my brush down my hand, to my wrist, my elbow, as if my arm were hollow, a paint-sucking straw. I can't help it.

"Another secret of good painting," my father instructs me, "is to paint in only one direction."

I don't want to do it that way. I want to move the brush all about as I wish, to go back and forth and perhaps to the side, to cover the thirsty wood with color as I feel like it.

"If you can't listen, we'll have to stop." I don't want to stop. My father *tsk*s his tongue. Though I am five, though this is the first time he's allowed me to help—none of this changes his appraisal. "That's all right," he says, saturating a rag with turpentine, rubbing my fingers, between my fingers, my wrist and arm. But I can tell he doesn't mean it. It isn't all right. I haven't learned the secret of good painting. I'm not fastidious or careful enough for science; my appetite refuses to be reined in by efficiency.

Yet I never doubted that girls could be scientists. I'd read Madame Curie's life story several times. I knew all about Elizabeth Blackwell, first woman M.D. west of the Rockies. Even the first dinosaur fossils were stumbled upon by a girl just about my age, playing in England roughly a century ago.

Oceanography, astronomy, physics, biology, anthropology: children are theoretical scientists without even trying. Though elementary-school science had been a drought I'd had to weather—the curriculum focused almost exclusively on pets and plants, leaves and pollen, the here and now of the natural world, which interested me not at all—I'd nonetheless managed to piece together a personal seminar with which to keep my love of science alive. My first unit was dinosaurs, though naming and categorizing their attributes—keeping track of which ate meat and which had spinal plates—soon proved too dusty and dry. Much more tantalizing was the fact that the maw of the past could be inferred from indecipherable remains scattered here and there, helter-skelter, waiting for serendipitous discovery and interpretation.

But animals never held my interest for long. From paleontology to archaeology was but a short step. Reading about King Tut and Schliemann's discovery of Troy, I announced my intention to join a dig—an activity that inextricably entwined science's theoretical and practical threads.

My father's steadfast belief that science belonged to the hands as much as the mind was reinforced by Mr. Brillman, my seventh-grade science teacher in Queens, a slightly paunchier, older version of my father. He wore dirty white lab coats two sizes too small and gave the impression of having ten arms, his desk a whirlwind of papers, his plaid shirt pocket a mess of pens and gauges, his pants drooping around his protruding belly. A boyish quality clung to both men; both had discovered in science and technology a personal fountain of youth. Their abiding belief in the redemptive promise of technology infused them with energy and endearing enthusiasm.

Anything, they believed, was possible, a let's-all-put-our-heads-together-and-I'm-sure-we-can-work-this-out mentality, which I found infectious.

But to their version of science I added my own, a personal science that sprang unbidden from questions I couldn't formulate aloud, questions that made my head hurt. What happened to you after you died? I'd ask myself in bed, when my parents made me turn out the flashlight by which I was reading. You never woke up. Never ever ever. What did that mean? Your children would have children who would have children who would have children, on and on into eternity, while you'd still be dead; they'd be going about their business and you'd be a footnote at first, then entirely forgotten. For some reason I always envisioned myself on a Ferris wheel in a dark amusement park, strapped into a cage suspended at the apogee of the orbit, shouting to my descendants running about below me, unable to make myself heard.

These questions, a form of autotorture, thrilled and terrified me, left me sweaty and exhausted. As a child, I never masturbated. That I could re-create, with my hands, the feeling I had when I sat on the banister watching the mailman sort the mail in the lobby of our apartment building, or when my bike went over a bump, never occurred to me. Instead, these dead-of-night questions were my stimulant.

For what fuels scientific inquiry but libido, a lusty, raucous combination of alchemy and metamorphosis? Things change dumbly into other things, elements escape their containers, boundaries blur; dinosaurs become petroleum, their footprints fossils; lakebeds end up deserts, volcanoes atolls. "It's fascinating!" I wrote in my diary. "I am breathing the same atoms created billions of years ago! They are never destroyed! WOW." Only science could take you to the frontier of possibility and then cover its tracks, leaving small, sometimes microscopic clues for the exceptionally observant. It was an orgy of plasticity, a big bang of disorder.

And technology was less science's handmaiden, as my father and Mr. Brillman assumed, than its antidote, invented and stoked by men who need to keep their hands busy to keep them out of their pants. The closer they came to unraveling science's allure, the more they had to control themselves, measure, calculate, deliberate, observe. They were afraid to jump in, to confront the hot and throbbing orgiastic heart of science—but I wasn't.

And neither, I hoped, was Miss Delray. Though tiny, she exuded charisma and soothing confidence. I was desperate to like her, and to have her like me. I wanted to become her disciple, to have her lead me where my father and Mr. Brillman couldn't.

I tried the best way I knew, by becoming a model student. Unfortunately, the curriculum made mincemeat of my intense desire to do well, to stand out, to be the star. Despite hours of studying, my grades were erratic. Science always caught me off-guard. I bounced around from *A*'s to *D*'s, doing well when I expected a poor grade, stumbling when I thought I'd done well. Graded on labs, surprised by quizzes, assigned lengthy and intricate projects, I struggled to maintain a *B* average, the minimum for entry into Honor Society. Miss Delray's class became the arena in which I was like everyone else: a run-of-the-mill, unremarkable student who worried about passing, who studied with not always stellar results.

Was this the ultimate affront from Miss Delray, from the subject—that I had to work at both my grades and my feelings toward her, both of which fluctuated wildly? "She's the biggest idiot ever!" I wrote one day, only to write the next, "Saw her in the supermarket. Such a sweet person. But a lousy teacher."

Perhaps my ambivalence arose from the confusion she caused in me, which I'd never before encountered. Take the eighth-grade science fair. Every other year, I'd depended on my father to help me with a project—he the chef, I the sous-chef. He'd make a design, find the materials, wield the saw, glue, and screwdriver, while I made tiny crosshatched pencil marks and held the nail. We never won, but our projects always looked sturdy and substantial; I was proud of them.

But some of Miss Delray's self-sufficiency must have rubbed off on me. "Why does he always have to come up with the ideas?" I wrote in my diary—as if my father had pleaded with me to let him help, when in reality I had always approached him. "This year I want to do something by myself." It seemed more important to fail on my own than succeed with my father. Anyway, I had the feeling she'd disqualify any project that hinted of parental help.

I ended up rigging a battery to some kind of switch: I have only the vaguest memory of it and the sense that it somehow resembled a mousetrap. It wasn't very good; Miss Delray didn't give it a second glance.

Even then I wasn't daunted. I still had my cancer journal to show Miss Delray—something I'd never shown to another adult, something that couldn't fail to impress her, to make her realize that despite my average grades and clumsiness with beakers and pipettes, I was a compatriot, a soulmate, a scientist at heart.

Ever since sixth grade, when we'd read a *Reader's Digest* story about Janice Babson, a Canadian girl who found herself feeling tired and was ultimately diagnosed with leukemia—the same disease that killed my maternal grandfather—I'd been compiling a notebook of articles about cancer clipped from newspapers and magazines. It was, I wrote in a ten-page introductory essay, "a mystery unsolved," the solution to which I would devote my professional life.

"By all means," Miss Delray had said, her interest piqued when I asked her, for the first time, if we could have an after-school conference. But as we stood together at her desk, leafing through the pages of my notebook, she seemed curiously uninterested, pausing hardly long enough to read my careful annotations:

"A new clue; maybe a vaccine to prevent the dreaded disease can make cancer of the blood as controllable and scarce as polio. Now, back to the drawing board!"

"Very interesting," she said when we reached the last page, speaking even more softly and slowly than she did in class.

I had hoped the notebook would spark a conversation, that we could talk about some of the ideas together, that she'd roll up her sleeves and work with me. But she found nothing remarkable in it. Instead, she asked me why I was so tense in her class.

"Me? Tense? Ha! I knew she didn't like me," I wrote that night in my diary. She'd probably intended to dispel my anxieties. But her unexpected question made me think twice before speaking, short-circuiting the very current that flowed so freely in English and cit. ed. All she accomplished was to make me more self-conscious, and to make me realize how little I liked her.

"When you pour a liquid into a container for measurement purposes," she said, "you may observe that there are two lines, one on top and one below. From which line do you measure?" This was a lesson about the meniscus, a word I remember to this day. I also remember the way she measured her words, the way she drew her tongue slowly across her lips as she poured the fluid from one flask to another, the sound of the liquid, the way she put the flask back on the counter, the sight of her short nail indicating the lip of fluid. I remember everything but from which line you measure.

Maybe it was ultimately her unflappability that jangled

me, set me off-balance. In her antiseptically neat classroom, science as I hoped it would be came to a screeching halt. She outdid even my father in her insistence on doing one thing at a time, on moving slowly and methodically, getting neither flustered nor elated. His devotion to cautious method arose in response to his natural, unbridled enthusiasm: Afraid to let himself go, he'd evolved a system to keep himself in check.

But she had no fear, she felt no allure. She simply enjoyed moving slowly.

"Dissection tomorrow," Miss Delray said at the end of class one April morning, rubbing her tiny hands together and looking at them, as if she half expected to see a spark within. The sheeps' eyes had finally arrived. Aproned and ready when we appeared the next day, she asked us to gather around her at the lab table to watch her technique. All her knives and utensils were laid out neatly, the eyes arranged in a pan like a casserole about to be popped into the oven. We jostled for position and a view, as the formaldehyde fumes snaked up our noses.

I was disgusted—and not merely by bloody tissue and ravaged sinew. This look-but-don't-touch dissection, the climactic lesson of the year, had nothing to do with my idea of science. It was too slow and deliberate, too mechanical, too recipe-based, a revolting combination of science, math, and home ec.

After watching for what seemed like hours as Miss Delray sliced, skinned, and separated, my lab partner and I were issued a tray with our own eye. We took it back to our seat and began. But it was already too late. The last drop of my interest in science, which had been slowly ebbing all year, circled the drain and disappeared with a resounding gurgle.

Only months before, I'd updated my cancer journal with its most exciting article yet—the surgeon general's report linking smoking and cancer. The last entry, a *Reader's Digest* article about DNA that I annotated, dates from April: "If we are able to unravel the code of life, a clue to cure cancer may be the next step. DNA is a major factor, the chain of molecules. So far, it is a deep dark mystery."

But it was a mystery that no longer engaged me. I abandoned my cancer journal, stowing it in a box for fossilization in a corner of my parents' basement, where I discovered it thirty years later. The only remaining dilemma posed by science was whether or not I'd be able to eke out a *B*– so I could qualify for Honor Society.

"Miss Delray is just about the worst teacher ever," I wrote. "Marks mean so damn much to her! She's giving out prizes if the marks and averages are in a certain range. Today we did nothing in class but for homework she assigned 2 chapters and a test tomorrow! I don't understand a damn thing! All I need is to fail now."

I didn't fail—I received an 88, which brought my average up to a creaky 80.33. I'd eked out the requisite *B*- after all.

Though I continued to take science through high

school, passing the physics regents (a statewide final exam) by the skin of my teeth, science and I broke up in eighth grade. For a while, after college, I considered a reconciliation: maybe I'd apply to medical school. But no sooner did I ponder all the makeup classes I'd have to take, all the math and statistics, all the Miss Delrays I assumed I'd encounter, than I changed my mind. Ultimately, my feelings then and now about the subject, too complicated for a diary entry, surfaced in an end-of-year poem for English, entitled "Science."

> Science is a mad professor with
> huge round glasses and curly hair
> bending over a test tube that is
> bubbling and steaming.
>
> Science is finding out that you can
> create the same bubbles and steam
> in your own home, using vinegar and
> baking soda.
>
> Science is being accurate and
> making sure you have exactly one
> milliliter of H_2O in a flask, and
> your pencil point is sharp enough
> to mark exactly one centimeter on
> your paper.
>
> When you hear a teacher say that
> she'd rather not go into the answer

to your question and to wait till
next year, you *know* it must be
science!

Science is learning that
superstition is ridiculous until
you see your teacher knocking wood
when you *finally* pass a science
test.

Science is learning about why we
get sick and why stars twinkle and
that we're not really made of sugar
n' spice but not why love makes the
world go round, cause love doesn't
have a formula.

If you are very logical, only then
can you be a scientist.

In Miss Delray's classroom, watching her finger the laboratory equipment and write in her painstaking script on the blackboard, I felt the first stirrings of a free-floating, nervous dread that would eventually contaminate my feelings about school. In Mr. Black's class I worried about achievement; in Mrs. Johnson's, about my social standing; but in science I became nervous about who I was. More accurately, I worried that I'd grow up to become another Miss Delray. It wasn't that she was mannish—she wasn't. She was simply sexless. Unsexy. Talk, the mad flow of ideas, was sexy. And Miss Delray couldn't, or wouldn't, talk, and nothing about her flowed madly.

She and I were polar opposites: I outer and she so inner focused that sometimes I wondered if she noticed us at all; if she needed us; if, faced with the prospect of a mass defection, she'd simply carry on in an empty classroom with whatever lesson she'd crafted for the day. She even laughed at her own jokes, unfazed when we didn't laugh. Like an inert element, she didn't interact with her surroundings.

Of what importance was science to Miss Delray? How did it fit into her life? In what ways did it comfort her? What need did it fill? I'd never thought to ask these questions of a teacher before, but ever since my *Moby Dick* report, when I'd glimpsed Mrs. Johnson listening to me with a look combining surprise, pleasure, and real anticipation, they cropped up unbidden. As Mrs. Johnson waxed richer, more complex, Miss Delray became flatter, more of a specimen. And science, the subject to which I'd been betrothed for years, my ticket to the future, my life's work, languished as my heart was slowly stolen by English, a suitor so plain I'd never before thought to notice him.

FEBRUARY 18:

School was fun for a change! We are going to the basketball game tomorrow. I love Mr. Black!

I couldn't share my blossoming crush on Mr. Black with anyone. Nearly every student and teacher found him snide, self-serving, obnoxious, full of himself, and contentious. Yet he made a habit of showering me with praise, finding me as special as my own father did. He singled me out for public glory, he enshrined me in his personal students' hall of fame. How could I resist?

We'd resumed our galloping course through American history after winter recess by studying the causes of the Civil War; by February, we were untangling Reconstruction. On current events days, we learned about corporate structure and labor unions. Each week, we had a test that combined essays with short answers. Looking through my papers now, I'm amazed to see that I once not only knew who Olive H. Kelley was (founder of the Patrons of Husbandry, forerunner of the Grange) but could write an entire essay about him.

Mr. Black was a memory-stretcher. I remember sitting in the living room with my notes, preparing for yet another test and feeling as if my saturated mind simply couldn't absorb another fact. Yet when I was presented with the questions in class, all the information surfaced in my brain, trickled down my arm, and flowed out of my pen. "Did you get that?" he'd ask, pausing for breath, gleefully smiling as we struggled to keep up with his dictation. "Will you remember it?" The more he talked, the faster I wrote, the more I retained and synthesized and repeated back to him.

"I want to meet his kids," I wrote in my diary. "I want to see him at home. I want to meet him in the bank. He's a pismire—and I like him."

"Pismire" was a term I'd picked up in English, where we were working our slow way through Thornton Wilder's play *On Borrowed Time.* Mrs. Johnson seemed content, these days, to while away entire periods having us simply read aloud from the script, the characters slowly emerging from the pages, becoming familiar, assuming seats among us as if they were new classmates. She didn't hurry us along, didn't seem to notice that we weren't really learning anything, that no one took notes or studied, that this had stopped being English class and had become something else.

We took turns reading parts, stopping whenever something arrested us or needed clarification. I was the character whom Rod's character called "pismire," a term that cracked us up and send us scurrying for the dictionary.

In the bull's-eye of the play is Grandfather, who climbs a tree and refuses to come down, thereby eluding death. But his obstinacy staves off not only his own demise but everyone else's, throwing the entire town out of joint.

Death up in a tree, like a stubborn, scared cat or a

mailman escaping a barking dog. The image did more than tickle our collective funny bone; it also embodied our nascent rebellion, our defiance, our egocentrism. The form of Grandfather's revolt spoke to us more than the content. For what did we suburban thirteen-year-olds know of death?

Most of our losses were at a generation's remove. One of my grandfathers, the one for whom I had been named, had died before my parents were married. His oil portrait, painted by a neighbor, hung in the dining room. Several times a year, according to the Jewish calendar, my mother lit a Yahrzeit candle, murmured a few prayers, and went to services, from which she returned hungry, headachy, and drawn.

Alice's grandfather had died a few months earlier. Beth had only one grandparent. There was a girl down the block, a fourth grader, who had leukemia. Anna's mother had died the month before I moved in; she had been in her thirties. Yet this fact never once came up in conversation. Her father had already remarried. In many ways these familial deaths were more remote than the spectacular death of JFK, which, catching us unawares at school, where we thought we were safe, precociously and permanently shattered our sense of complacency and faith.

Had Mrs. Johnson recently suffered a loss in her family? About her personal life she was exceedingly discreet: I don't know if she had children, where she lived, what kind of car she drove. Friendly but distant, she kept her own counsel and didn't encourage confessions and soul-searching discussions, either in class or during private conferences about our work and progress.

I can't swear that she had mortality on her mind, but now, having turned forty myself, I imagine that she did, that she felt its palpable presence like a current of arctic air snaking into a closed-up house through a tiny crack in the attic. Why else would we have moved directly from *On Borrowed Time* to *Our Town*—yet another Wilder play about death, this time from the point of view of those who have died.

How we ached with Emily, the young girl who perished in childbirth, as she journeyed from the cemetery back to her own kitchen, only to see how life is squandered. How we enjoyed the Stage Manager, with his brisk way of moving the action along, flouting dramatic conventions such as set changes and intermission by placing them center stage.

More plays! we told Mrs. Johnson. This was fun. Yet according to our syllabus, it was time for our unit on poetry. Oh, no, we groaned, not poetry! How many times had we compressed seventeen syllables into a three-line haiku; how many rhymes could we force, how many rhythms mangle? Poetry was inevitably the worst part of English, those dreary textbooks with chapters on meter and imagery, the poems used as illustrative examples, either as elementary as Mother Goose or too obscure to crack. More plays! we demanded, or we'd climb a tree like Grandfather and refuse to get down.

But Mrs. Johnson deftly outsmarted us, avoiding an out-and-out mutiny by proposing a clever compromise. Move on to poetry we must, but she'd preserve the theme. "Death Comes Alive!" she wrote gleefully on the board one morning to begin class. Then she distributed a sheaf of mimeographed papers on which she had duplicated the greatest poems in the English language about death, a home-cooked collection on which to cut our poetical teeth.

This happened so quickly we didn't have time to protest, to argue that it wasn't death we were interested in, of course, it was the plays we enjoyed, the act of reading, of acting them out. But too late; our poetry unit was launched. We found ourselves sitting and listening as Mrs. Johnson read aloud to us from her makeshift anthology: "Death be not proud," "Ozymandias," "To an Athlete Dying Young," "Crossing the Bar," "Because I Could Not Stop for Death," "Poor soul, the centre of my sinful earth."

She fingered her beads as she read, her voice thin and altogether unmemorable. After each poem she removed her eyeglasses and stuck the end of one earpiece in her mouth, waiting a moment while her eyes refocused, as if the page had swallowed her. "You're still here?" she seemed to say with a kindly but faintly admonishing smile, she the host who'd gone up to bed and changed into her nightgown and robe, only to come down for a glass of milk and find us in the kitchen, guests who'd innocently but unthinkingly overstayed our welcome.

There we sat, twenty-five pairs of eyes waiting for her

to say something about the poem she'd just read, as we were well within our rights to expect—this was English class, after all—but she'd lost track of herself and regarded us as trespassers. It was as if the act of reading had dematerialized her, as if she'd been transported like a character on *Star Trek* into another dimension and we had to wait for her to beam herself back down, for her molecules to reassemble and remind her who and where she was.

She roused herself not to ask a question but to make a comment: "Listen to that wording: 'Then, soul, live thou upon thy servant's loss.' Isn't that beautiful? How does it make you feel? What does it call to mind?" she asked in her dreamy way. Slowly, we'd wend our way through the poem, taking our time, starting at the beginning, examining each word, each phrase, being asked what it made us think of, how it made us feel. There was, apparently, no wrong answer. She listened to everyone, to all suggestions, though some, it was clear, caught her short, made her look inward before answering.

If school was like learning to dance, we were used to the two-step: first them, then us. First Mr. Black prepared his lecture, Miss Delray her experiment, Mrs. Villard her equation, and then they presented it to us. Their creative work, their behind-the-scenes preparation, had already taken place, in private; in class they were merely going through rehearsed motions. They had all the answers and were merely waiting, disguising their impatience, for us to discover them. Engaged as we were in separate activities, performance and absorption, a gulf separated us from our teachers.

But Mrs. Johnson consulted no notes, no answer key, no procedural workbooks, only the poems themselves. We never had the feeling that she'd studied them the night before and was marking time, waiting for us to give her the answers she expected. Instead, she was very much reading *with* us.

She was infinitely patient. "There are a lot of *l* sounds in that line: 'Then, soul, live thou upon thy servant's loss,'" one of us thought to comment.

"Oh, yes," Mrs. Johnson would say, offhandedly. "That's called alliteration." When someone thought to comment on the fact that death becomes a person in Dickinson's "Because I Could Not Stop for Death," Mrs. Johnson told us casually, "Oh, yes, that's something called personification"—these terms not discrete entities that could be surgically removed from the poem itself but intrinsic to it, woven from its very fiber. Yes, she implicitly told us, poetry had a lexicon, a vocabulary, a modus operandi, certain conventions, but never let this take precedence over the fact that poetry speaks most urgently to the heart.

When we finished the first collection of poems, Mrs. Johnson prepared another, this one featuring works by Whitman, Gray, Rossetti, Brooke, and biblical psalms. Again we absorbed them rather than study them, became immersed in them, as in a foreign language. Mrs. Johnson became less recognizably a teacher than her own student; and Zen-like, we learned because we weren't taught.

That our activities in English verged on the subversive dawned on us all. I'm sure Mrs. Johnson had to obtain some kind of departmental clearance to proceed with her plan, but she undoubtedly misrepresented what was happening; otherwise, who would have approved? Like co-conspirators, we adopted an air of secrecy. We hoarded our unit and our death-related readings.

And the covert, almost clandestine climate was deeply appealing. To Alice, Denise, Beth, and me, the discovery of poetry was like stumbling upon a code we couldn't wait to crack. We loved the referential aspect of literature, the way one poem influenced and echoed another like atoms in a reaction chamber, causing ripples and confluences that spread for hundreds of years. We loved this new language stripped of everything but its essentials, the opposite of everyday speech, of the language of family life. It was the real thing, the pure It. We were transfixed by the abounding paradoxes: that so few words could say so much, that writing an immortal poem about death's bleak, inescapable finality was an escape from, a triumph over, a negation of death.

Maybe the looming shadow of our next report card woke Mrs. Johnson from her trance. For the first time in weeks she made an actual assignment—one so orthodox and old-fashioned that it stunned us into submission: we had to select a poem from the anthology and memorize it.

I didn't waste a moment wondering which poem to choose: "Ozymandias" exerted an almost mystical appeal.

It spoke to me, perhaps because becoming an archaeologist was my second announced profession, predating even my interest in medical research.

I loved the fact that its rhymes were obscured. I loved the words "antique," "trunkless," and "visage." But the twelfth line cut through me like a cold blade: "Nothing beside remains," intones the traveler after the statue has his say.

I can still recite the poem as I was called to that winter. The words come haltingly but steadily, each leading inexorably to the one that follows.

For our next assignment we assembled our own anthology of death poems, illustrating them with drawings or with pictures cut from magazines. Finally, as the unit and the winter drew to a close, we were asked to write one of own. I titled mine "Hope."

> Someone must turn the hourglass over!
> For somehow the grains of sand gently slide
> through the tiny space . . .
>
> Someone must watch the grains of sand.
> And someone must see the gap that remains
> As the young sand drops and nothingness remains
> Until the glass is turned over once more;
> Till life and love begin once more.
> The old grains of sand, now newly replaced,
> Can rest in peace, dream and hope
> That someone is still turning the hourglass.

I was dissatisfied with my effort, although Mrs. Johnson gave me an *A*-. It wasn't what I meant to say. The poem sounded too dumbly hopeful, when I wanted to convey the opposite, that hope had to be wrested away from the brink, from the precipice. If anything, I wanted to show how perilously close we were to oblivion. I meant it more as *a* hope, not generic hope.

But words had a life of their own, and I couldn't sculpt them, especially words that tried to rhyme and stay in some kind of rhythm. Beth's poem was better, so was Alice's. Denise wrote a haiku, three spare, elegant lines that were much more in keeping with what I wanted to say. Hers was the best, I thought. The four of us spent hours poring over our efforts. As much as I wanted mine to shine, the fact that it didn't, that I could defer to Denise, that I could acknowledge hers as more accomplished, surprised me. In all other subjects, a less than perfect score made me itch all over, inducing a near-bodily discomfort, as if I had bugs in my clothes. It was almost physically unbearable.

But this poetry unit infused me with a new spirit. Individual achievement was only a small step in a very long journey. There was so much else to do—read, comment, analyze, inch a tentative way toward understanding—all this as much a part of the process as actual composition. And transforming everything else was the web of friendship we spun as we went, our recognition that we were a community brought together by something bigger and more enduring than all of us.

Mrs. Johnson made an anthology of our poems. We were all awestruck, I remember, thumbing through the mimeographed booklet, to see the quality of the work we had produced. Even Rod and the other boys had taken the assignment to heart. The poems were serious, full of endeavor. It seemed miraculous.

The entire unit seems a miracle now. Though our minds were mired in our social lives and report card grades, we spent two months pondering "And death shall be no more: Death, thou shalt die"—a paradox as complicated and demanding as any in math or science, as hard to work your mind around and digest. Just when you thought you understood it, had trapped it on the microscope slide, it changed shape and squirmed away.

Still, the words were comforting, they were profound, they were heartfelt, they made a difference. A poem, Mrs. Johnson taught us, isn't something you read, use up, and discard—"There, I'm done with that," like those eyeballs on the dissection tray. Poetry hung around in your head long after you read it, like an inextinguishable flame.

This was Mrs. Johnson's final gift: the most private of our teachers, she allowed us to glimpse her at her most unselfconscious, and ended up the most exposed. The words she read tumbled out of her mouth like tiny but powerful boomerangs, cutting through the air above us—we could feel the air currents they set in motion—on their trajectory through the room and back to her. She let us watch her welcome them home, let us watch as they comforted her; it was almost like watching her bathe. But we didn't have to avert our eyes. She invited us to see the ways in which poetry was a balm to her soul, to see how it mattered to her, that to her it was a matter of life or death. That it could save us as well.

LUNCH

My social life, however, seemed beyond saving. If anything, it grew more muddled as the year went on. At the beginning of the year, I'd had only to worry about where I'd sit each day at lunch. That Alice and Beth considered me a permanent fixture at their table, ensconced in their constellation of friends, was something I couldn't at first take for granted. Weeks went by before I felt comfortable sitting down as if I belonged with them.

I'd joined a group of girls who had been together the previous year. Eighth grade, however, was a time of reshuffling, a time to weed out undesirables and solidify ties among those of us who survived the purge. With Borgia-like ruthlessness, we banished one girl to the corner of our table, and ultimately to another table entirely, thanks to "Plan X," a top-secret strategy Alice and I cooked up, which involved a staged fight, forged notes, and bogus meetings. At any second, of course, such a plan could have been formulated to dispose of me.

We swam in treacherous waters. Alliances formed during class lasted until the bell rang, collapsed in the corridor, and flourished anew in the cafeteria. There was so much to keep track of—who went home with whom, who spoke to whom on the phone last night and for how long, how many parties and bar and bat mitzvahs you were invited to, how many times you were asked to dance, what the raised eyebrow or the phony grin meant. No throwaway piece of body language, no shrug or tic, was beneath notice or escaped scrutiny and endless analysis.

We called it our "social life," but it was more social Darwinism, these hyperpersonal connections that crackled like a current, electrifying whatever room we happened to find ourselves in. Eighth grade was nothing less than a survival-of-the-fittest safari into the undergrowth of friendship, as emotionally cutthroat and competitive as anything Mr. Black could devise.

Thanks to my catholic taste in friends, I felt particularly vulnerable to finding myself sacrificed. In our circle, I was the one with the most varied, even disparate, friendships. Like an octopus's, each of my eight arms reached out in radically different directions. With Ilene, the chorus accompanist, I exchanged daily four-page, single-spaced typewritten fantasies spun from the most recent episode of *The Man from U.N.C.L.E.;* with Barbara I played tennis and went bowling; with Linda I talked about clothes and I still kept in touch with friends from Queens, with whom I talked sports.

"Grow up!" Beth, Alice, and Denise each told me with disparaging looks. Hadn't I yet realized that it was time to jettison extraneous interests and the friendships they spawned, to decide who I was? No one could be friends with everyone. From every side—not simply parents and teachers, but my girlfriends as well—I felt an increasing pressure to declare myself, to narrow myself down, as if growing up was a journey for which I was dangerously overpacked.

Yet I wasn't ready to specialize, even as I grew increasingly ashamed of my desire for diversity. The worst moment was when I inadvertently misdelivered notes one morning in homeroom, and the four-page paean to the indescribable cuteness of David McCallum fell into Alice's rather than Ilene's hands.

Alice returned it, after reading it, with a withering look, one which suggested that maybe she didn't know me so well after all. And then I had to write her another note, explaining that this fantasy was really one I indulged in for Ilene's sake, not my own.

In other words, I told lies—white lies, I hoped—to wriggle out of tight situations, explain myself, put my actions in the best possible light, hoping to alienate no one. And when the truth invariably came out, I resorted to more lies, to sleight of hand, to hair-splitting exegesis, to assure everyone that I was still who they thought I was. A budding diplomat, I learned to appease.

"Why can't we all be friends?" I wanted to say but knew I couldn't. The answer had to do with something I didn't yet understand. In one sense, Alice and Beth and Denise seemed strong and I was weak; they were discerning and I was indiscriminate; they were pure and I was corrupt. More accurately, I think they were simply biologically ahead of me, acting on a jealousy that was primarily sexual in nature, something I had yet to experience.

Boys presented an even bigger problem. Though we sat intermingled in class, in the cafeteria we self-segregated, sitting at adjacent lunch tables just far enough apart to overhear each other's conversation and exchange nasty retorts.

Why Alice and Beth wanted to have anything to do with the boys mystified me. No sooner did they set foot in the cafeteria, where they were free from a teacher's watchful eye, able to congregate in an ungainly mob, than they were transformed. Even Eddie and Rod, on whom I lavished huge crushes, and who in class were alternately solicitous, funny, and comradely, turned during lunch into snide, sniping monsters, reduced to making fun of my blouse, Ilene's eyebrows, Alice's hair.

Even worse, by midyear our coed social life began overspilling the confines of the cafeteria.

JANUARY 3, 1965:

Beth is having a party. If I go, what happens if I don't dance again? It seems like it's just at the party no one likes me. But right after and before, everyone loves me! I just hope I dance. I'll look so damned retarded, I swear. I ain't expecting too much, I'm not even sure I really want to go.

Beth's party was tethered to no special occasion, such as her birthday. Sadly for me, boy-girl parties now took place at whim, whenever somebody felt like it. "I'm thinking of having a party," someone would say offhandedly at lunch, everyone's eyes perking up but mine, the idea gathering momentum and taking off like a rocket ship. The opportunities multiplied: to buy a new dress, try a new lipstick and hairstyle, banish parents if only for a few hours, pretend the house was ours, invite boys over to lurk in the corners, put on new records, and see what happened. Something always happened.

Was I the only one who dreaded them, the only one who felt dismay at the thought of what to wear and how to set her hair? Like a looming cit. ed. test, the prospect of a party cast a dark shadow over my days. But a test I knew I could ace; parties were ungraded, yet I always seemed to fail.

At least no one expected me to throw a party. My family's ranch-style house, with an unfinished basement, failed the only prerequisite for hosting: parents and party would have to exist on the same level, and this was entirely untenable.

Beth's split-level was made for parties, the den located in the back, down one flight of stairs from the kitchen and two from the bedrooms, where her parents and sisters were exiled. Etiquette was suspended during parties; we were free to ignore adults and siblings, to think of them as invisible, or treat them as servants whose job it was to open the door, hang coats, and scurry around refilling bowls of chips and supplying soda.

"There's Anna!" we'd shriek when someone appeared at the top of the stairs, each of us accorded a debutante's entrance. We flocked around her, admiring her new shoes, sniffing her perfume, touching her dress, complaining about our hair, which had a mind of its own.

I felt awkward in my party clothes, a by-product of my parents' refusal to let me grow gracefully into adolescence. Instead, I had to claw my way out. Each of my requests—for a bra, nylons, makeup, a dress in a bright color with a little bit of flair—met with staunch resistance, led to horrible fights, left me crying hot tears of desperation. Their enemy was biology, their efforts to prolong my childhood nothing more than a finger in the dike. But the knowledge that they were sure to lose—that my hormones would triumph no matter how many times they forbade me to use hair spray—didn't dissuade them.

My friends had no such parental obstacle course to run. In close-fitting dresses, lipstick and eye shadow, perfume and high heels, they were entirely at home—this their true appearance, everything else a temporary disguise. Transformed, they shook off the ties that bound them to me. In school, in each other's bedrooms, Anna, Beth, Alice, and I were confederates; now I felt abandoned, our bonds dissolved. It was every girl for herself.

The boys always came late, though they didn't so much arrive as appear, as if they'd been lurking in the corners, by the record player or the table with the soda and chips, and simply coalesced when the lights were sufficiently dimmed. Someone put on a record, turned off a light. Whatever food appeared—bowls of soggy popcorn and potato chips, sodas—was scarfed down in an instant. No matter how large the room, we clustered like bees in a hive, climbing all over one another, close enough to feel each other's clammy skin. The hi-fi blared. Beth and Alan were dancing. Alice and Peter were making out in the corner. Laura hadn't stopped talking to Mark. Adam phoned; he and some friends from a neighboring school were coming to crash the party. Anna's bra strap broke.

I welcomed these distractions; they diverted me from my agony. Each new song was a torment, especially the slow ones, which became more frequent as the night drew on. Wouldn't someone ask me to dance? If only I had bad skin or a weight problem, I could slink from view. My problems—my height and my hair—resisted camouflage. I was the only one unable to claim a single component of female beauty. None of us fit the composite: five feet four, bubbly, blond, and athletic. But Anna had the perkiness, Beth achieved the perfect pageboy, Alice was the right height. I, on the other hand, was too tall, too clumsy, and my hair was an uncontrollable frizzy mop. I'd sat under the hair dryer until I thought my scalp had melted, but now my hair had broken free of its constraints and was crimping like crazy.

Just one dance, I would plead silently as the evening dragged on, just one dance so I could salvage my self-respect—even though I couldn't dance to save my life.

Wouldn't even one boy hear my desperate cry? How many times would I be forced to lip-synch rather than stare at Anna or Beth digging her fingers into Rod's or Michael's clammy back? How many trips to the bathroom could I make?

But it wasn't simply the ordeal of standing around feeling as attractive as the pole lamp; or the miserable realization that the degree to which every boy was steadfastly ignoring me rendered me as conspicuous as a scantily dressed go-go dancer on *Shindig*. What brought me close to tears was the knowledge that this boded badly for my future. I was destined for spinsterhood.

When the doorbell finally rang, eons later, I groaned along with everyone else, though I knew it was my father, who'd come to rescue me—and not a moment too soon. He made small talk with Beth's father while I hunted for my coat and rounded up the friends he'd agreed to drive home.

They crowded into the back seat as if they were drunk, shrieking into their hands, stage-whispering and giggling like the typical teenagers they were, reliving the party's unforgettable moments while I sat up front, sober in my mother's seat. My father tried to talk to my friends, determined not to be treated like a "chauffeur," disappointed with the one-word answers my friends offered. Patiently he'd sit in the driveway until my friend disappeared into her house, and I knew I'd hear about it later if she forgot to say thank you.

"Have a good time?" my father would unfailingly ask when everyone had been deposited and we were on our way home. Under his jacket he was wearing his pajama top, and his hat was positioned far back on his head, not at its usual crisp angle; if I had stopped thinking about myself for one second, I would have realized how tired he was, how much of an imposition it was to ask him to come at midnight and shepherd us home. But none of us questioned our right to a social life, or to our parents' participation in this effort.

"Yeah," I'd say, trying to sound enthusiastic. There was no way I could let on, especially to him, what a social failure I'd turned out to be. How could I let him know that his solicitude and tutelage had left me so ungainly?

He'd pull into the garage, open the front door for us, turn off the light he'd left on in the kitchen. Together we'd walk down the hall to the bedrooms; in the foyer, where we could hear my mother's and my sister's breathing, he'd kiss me good night and hug me slightly longer than I wanted him to. I knew he was thinking about how fast I was growing up. The weight of his expectations, of his misinformed assumption that I'd one day be married and have children of my own, unhinged me; I had to find some solitude in which to collapse.

In my bedroom, I'd squeeze out a few tears and write some self-pitying pages in my diary. "All the boys keep talking to me, kid me, walk with me, and no one dances with me! Everyone else had a blast. When we were talking it was okay. But Anna had to tell the boys to dance with me. I felt very embarrassed. Why is God doing this to me? Please, no more!"

In my heart I knew I wasn't hated or actively disliked. I wasn't an outcast. If anything, I had a very secure berth smack in the middle of the social order. There were, I knew, plenty of girls beneath me who would have cut off their hands to be invited to Beth's party. But I also knew that there was an upper stratum, girls who weren't necessarily in our classes but whom we met in gym and saw at lunch, girls who were "popular" and had boyfriends, some in high school. I also knew that some boys liked me, though not the ones I wanted to, and that made me better off than the girls whom no boys liked.

As much as I disparaged my looks, I knew I wasn't disfigured or misshapen; people didn't flee from me, boys liked to talk to me, even if they didn't want to hold me close. Anyway, physical appearance wasn't all that counted. "Personality" mattered too. But in this department I probably had too much. I overpowered. I overwhelmed boys. I didn't know how to be coy or to flirt. Everything I wanted was written all over my face.

"Not everyone gets married," my mother would occasionally tell me in a peculiar tone of voice, as if she'd half considered staying single herself. But she knew all about social pressure, and I did too. In a couples' world, I'd be perennially out of step. Could anything be sadder than facing my life with a brave but thin smile while the rest of the world melted into each other's arms?

In bed, replaying moments from the party, I tried to picture myself in a dark corner with a boy—Rod? Eddie? His identity didn't really matter. While the party swirled around us, we were making out, his face nuzzling my neck, his fingers in my hair. . . .

But I couldn't make it work. For even as he put his hand on my thigh, I felt a spectral version of myself rise out of my body and take her place with my friends who were watching us, who were secretly smirking at the incongruous sight: I was much too big to sit on anyone's lap. I was making a spectacle of myself, as my mother would say.

It was hopeless. Even in my most private fantasies, I couldn't stay in my own skin. I only knew how to be a spectator, not an actor. Nothing would ever happen to me. I was useless as a girl.

JANUARY 4:

I realized I had a gr8 time at Beth's party. Really. I don't really like any of the boys. And if any of the girls there did, and vise versa, enjoy! Every one will be married in the end. I'm not hated, I'm even liked by Rod. Not like he likes Anna, though, but in his own way. I had a blast!

Of course, I didn't so much "realize" as retrospectively mandate—after a night's sleep and multiple conversations with my friends—that I'd had a good time. The constitutional equanimity I'd inherited from my father always appeared at the critical juncture, saving me when drowning seemed imminent.

But no optimism would save me from acknowledging that I had three basic boy problems. One was purely physical: I was too tall. Of the three boys I especially liked, all were shorter than I was, and two, my favorites, were much shorter. I could have smothered them.

That none of them could ever act as if he liked me—by inviting me to dance with him at a bar mitzvah or party—was obvious to anyone with eyes; the discrepancy in our heights was simply too extreme. With a just-the-facts-ma'am terseness, I recorded in my diary the puny contents of each party's dance card the same way I had once kept track of Yankee games: "Not one dance tonight," or "Just Paul," referring to the only eighth-grade boy taller than I who at each occasion felt it his obligation to imperceptibly nod at me, lead me to the dance floor, and put his arms around me as passionately as he would embrace a laundry bag.

"Oh, well," I'd conclude after each disappointing entry, "it's just because I'm so tall. I still know I looked good; everyone said so." The shame I held at bay was as much for the boys as for myself. I imagined they must have suffered for their shortness as much as I did for my height. In the meantime, I prayed that the growth spurt encoded in their genes would unleash the feelings they harbored for me in their hearts.

My second problem was more complex:

JANUARY 7:

Ted asked me to go steady. Then he said no man is an island, but he is. I felt very sorry for him so I wrote him a letter.

Ted was the smartest and most physically and socially uncomfortable boy in our grade. He'd begun writing me notes months before—he had a beautiful, almost girlish handwriting—letting me know that he thought I was special. Still, his invitation to go steady, to accept and wear his silver ID bracelet, surprised me. That I had to turn him down was so obvious I didn't even mention it in my diary. He'd be a social liability. Even he understood that because I cared about my social standing I could never accept him. Everyone knew that it was worse to go out with a boy no one liked than not to go steady at all—the latter indicating bad luck, the former inexcusably bad judgment.

My last problem was Rod. Nowhere in my diary could I confide my true feelings toward him. He was smart, funny, arrogant, crass, rude, irreverent, irremediably self-centered—and dangerously impulsive: at a party, he pushed a girl down after she slapped him. "God did I hate him at that moment!" I wrote, joining the chorus of my friends who regularly disparaged him, found him beneath contempt. "But I think I still like him."

In fact, I loved him. Innocently, I'd stepped into one of society's most enduring roles for women: armed with endless patience and X-ray vision, I alone could disregard his swagger, see past it to his core, where he was kind, loving, and vulnerable. He acted like a monster only because he was insecure—insecure in a way that I alone could assuage.

His chief recommendation, the one that kept me pining for him day after interminable day, wasn't what I could do for him but what he could do for me: reaffirm, with each snub, my conviction that he'd never like me, never in a million years. Bluntly put, I wasn't "his type"—which meant, most superficially, that I was tall and had auburn hair, and he was after short, perky, track 2 blondes. I managed to select for a crush the one boy for whom I truly *was* too much: too tall, too smart, too ambitious, too competitive. "I saw him with his mother when we were in the car today," I wrote in my diary. "I heard him use the word 'honey'—not to me, of course."

I knew he had some kind of feelings about me, but they were complicated, inchoate feelings, at a time when I craved directness and simplicity. Either a boy asked you to go steady—which meant he accosted you near your locker before homeroom, standing close enough so you could smell his breath and see the whiteheads around his nostrils and mouth, and gave you his thick silver ID bracelet to wear on your wrist—or he didn't. Rod never came close to making me such an offer. Yet he also never once made fun of me the way he did of nearly every other girl in our class. For whatever reason, I had an unspoken exemption.

This exemption, however, brought anguish as well as delight. Was there no boy on earth who would find my specialness something to embrace, to want more of?

Well, in all honesty, there was Steve. He'd been in several of my classes for the past year and a half, and I'd never paid him more than glancing attention. He was about as tall as I was, a big advantage, and best of all, he occasionally asked me to dance at parties. He was friendly, and he was smart, but not as smart as Rod or me. According to all my girlfriends, he was the answer to my prayers. Alice predicted he'd ask me to go steady, which he never did, yet that he liked me I never doubted.

He was the boyfriend who would have made life easier for me, if I could have brought myself to like him. He liked me for the wrong reasons, which seemed worse than Rod stiffing me for the right reasons. To Steve, I was a regular girl. He couldn't possibly have appreciated what was inside. Rod, I was convinced, *knew* me; knew what he was rejecting. It was a crucial difference.

By spring, my feelings had changed considerably. At the last moment, against all odds, Steve asked me to go on a date. That night I wrote in my diary, "I want to tell you this before something spoils it. Steve asked me to the school play tonight. He asked me after science, just after the bell rang. Dammit, I was so damn happy, you can't believe it! I'll set my hair and wear my suit. I can't wait—he's the greatest kid! I'm so *excited!*"

Love to the rescue. So great was my relief and rapture that I didn't even mind that Rod asked Alice. We all sat together, and the play, a satire of the school and all the faculty, was entirely diverting.

"I never had such a great time," I wrote the next day. "Conversation came so easily. What if he doesn't like me anymore? Please do, I want this to happen again and again. I love love, it's so beautiful. After he asked me, my heart was beating, I was flushed, I could feel the envious stares, but it was me, Roberta Israeloff, sitting next to Steve Miller, a boy! I was so proud. I think he likes me. Please do, please ask me again."

Steve did indeed call again; in fact, two days after our date, he came over to my house and we played catch, with my hardball. "He was impressed," I wrote. I could always rely on my athletic prowess to impress boys, not only because they expected so little from girls but also because I was truly good.

Yet I was far from mastering the vagaries of dating.

JUNE 11:

Why does everything with me turn out to be cockeyed? All day I waited for Steve to ask me to the school dance. So tonight, we started talking about it, and he asks me if I bought a ticket, and I said no. Then he said he was going to ask me this afternoon but someone told him that I bought a ticket already. I said no. He asked me if I wanted to go with Ted and I said no, and then he gave me a real great smile. So I don't really know if he really asked me or not. I think he did, but I'm not sure. Why couldn't he just have asked me? It's so simple *that way.*

It took me two days to determine that yes, Steve had indeed asked me, that I could relax: I'd be at the dance with my other friends; my lack of a date wouldn't brand me as a social outcast.

JUNE 18:

I don't know, something must be drastically wrong with me. I don't like Steve. I love Eddie. I couldn't wait to leave though tonight. It was awful. I would have been better off going stag! I love Eddie. I had a good time. Steve was dancing with me and Ted was following me and Mr. Black was there.—When will I ever find the right boy? Will I ever?

JUNE 19:

I'm so depressed, I don't know what to do with Steve. I just wish I could never see him again. Ever. I hate him.

I didn't really hate him. It only seemed as if his attentions—the fact that he now wanted to spend time with me, come over to my house, walk me home from school, wait for me at my locker, call me on the phone—repulsed me.In fact, the loathing was self-directed. Until he made his intentions clear, he wasn't real to me, and I was free to think I liked him. But the very awakening of his appetite killed mine. More accurately, it pointed out the nonexistence of my own appetite, the fact that I had no emotional apparatus in place to determine how I actually felt about him. Quite simply, I had no capacity for liking him back. I wasn't ready for a social life. Apparently, I wanted only things I couldn't have, and things that came too easily, well, they were the worst of all.

For ten more years I was stuck in a dreary pattern, liking boys only until they liked me and then feeling revulsion, remaining faithfully devoted to boys who would never care for me. My method of flirting, I realize now, was to reveal tiny chunks of Rutherford, as if he were a monster chained up in a dark, dank basement—first a toe, then a foot, then a leg—to see how my boyfriend reacted. Some, sensing the monster's power even behind bars, were scared; others were repulsed; yet others welcomed him, embraced him. I distrusted *them* most of all.

When I met David, the man I married, I abandoned my usual strategy in favor of opening the dungeon door all the way. "I'm going out of town this weekend," I'd announce on Friday night after a delicious Chinese dinner he'd prepared for me in his closet of a kitchen—one of countless times I seized the agenda, asserted my independence with what felt like unaccustomed ruthlessness, catered to my own whims and needs, without thinking for a moment of his.

"I'm not ready to make a commitment to you," I told him every time he brought up the subject. "Don't rush me." He acquiesced, yet suffered no diminishment. He didn't flinch when I trotted out the beast of my appetite—and, even more hideous, the beast of my indecision, who couldn't make up her mind, who couldn't plumb her own desires, who needed to temporize endlessly.

"I'll wait," he said, meeting my self-interest head-on, accepting it while letting me know he wished things were otherwise. We've been married nearly twenty years.

Though I swore each time I was pregnant that I was carrying a girl, I ended up with two boys, who are, in my mother's words, "all boy." Rough-and-tumble, full of energy and competition, they love nothing more than to mix it up as loudly and physically as we'll allow. It's thanks to Rutherford, I think, that they're so boyish. Yet they have many feminine attributes. They love to talk, and they have words for what they're feeling as well as thinking. They're physically affectionate, even in public.

Most tellingly, as Ben turns thirteen, he's begun to step into himself—to fill out his body, to feel more comfortable in his skin—at precisely the age I began to step out of mine. All the confidence I lost or learned to put away he's now drawing in, marshaling, learning to wield. He can't help but speak his mind—not to do so isn't an option on his personal palette, a quality I admire and envy even more—yet so finely are his antennae attuned to the feelings of others that his comments routinely catch people off-guard.

"Actually, he's a little too sensitive," Ben's third-grade teacher once told me. "You must have spent an awful lot of time with him, talking to him, when he was a baby."

I did. I still do. I'm probably less self-conscious with my children than I am with anyone else on earth. Into their laps I've poured all the attributes that had been bestowed upon me, generously but in separate boxes, labeled "boy" and "girl." So far they've moved from strength to strength: they have their problems, but not ones that arise from having a shadowy presence needing to be locked in a closet, banished to the underworld.

Will Ben be popular? I wonder, as he dresses for a party he's invited to. Lately, he's been taking his time in front of the mirror, requesting certain types of shirts, dropping girls' names during dinner conversation. He slips a hand into his pants pocket and runs his fingers through his hair with such masculine aplomb that I wonder if his food has been pumped with hormones. When he lets me hug him good-bye, I feel, beneath his T-shirt, the smooth, damp back of all the boys at all the basement parties to which I was ever invited.

MARCH 7:

> The Free Silver movement is a fake. Free Silver is the cow-bird of the reform movement. It waited until the nest had been built by the sacrifices and labour of others, and then laid its eggs in it. . . . The People's Party has been betrayed. . . . No party that does not lead its leaders will ever succeed.
>
> —William Jennings Bryan
> Campaign of 1896

"Cow-bird? What's a cow-bird?"

Mr. Black grinned demonically. The mimeographed sheets containing the assignment for our second reaction paper were being distributed and hadn't yet reached those of us in the back rows, but already the class was abuzz, awash in anxiety.

"As in the last paper, which I've just returned," he began, "you have to either agree or disagree with this quotation and explain why. And don't ask me, Mr. Miller, how long it has to be," he said, glaring at Steve, whose hand was in the air. "I don't believe in length requirements. A paper should be as long as it takes to make a persuasive argument. It's due a week from today."

Reaction papers were Mr. Black's climactic assignment, the *sine qua non* of his course, the defining moment for each of his students, which made child's play of every previous essay test, campaign journal, and book report.

These papers required, he never tired of telling us, a unique combination of skills, to interpret, research, analyze, organize, argue, and express ideas. Critical thinking was what he was trying to teach us, cit. ed. a hybrid subject that grafted precise scientific methodology onto ideas.

"I've been assigning reaction papers since the year I began teaching," Mr. Black had said to begin class just a few minutes earlier, holding the first set of corrected papers in his hand. "I've given a few *A* minuses, some *A*'s, but never an *A* plus."

He started walking slowly toward me and handed me my paper. On the title page was "*A*+, Excellent," in red pen.

Staring at the paper as if it had descended from heaven, I tried to assimilate what this meant. Though I'd long become accustomed to success in this class, this was the mother of all successes, the pinnacle of achievement. At first I felt nothing but pure relief and sweet vindication. So thoroughly had this assignment obsessed me that I'd insisted my mother drive me to the library in a neighboring town, which boasted a superior reference department. There, day after day, Saturday and Sunday too, I combed through obscure periodicals and books, taking painstaking notes, typing up nearly five full pages of single-spaced text, arguing that by the late 1880s the conflict between industrial and agrarian America had ended, industry emerging victorious. Back and forth in my diary I'd debated whether the paper was a success.

Yes, it had all been worth it.

Yet I could feel in the room, as I hadn't detected earlier in the term, a slight simmering resentment directed my way. Some of my friends had received *A*'s; why exactly had mine merited that extra "plus"? Had I truly earned my bonus, or was I simply following the trajectory on which I had been launched back in the fall?

But at the moment, I didn't have time to sift through these questions. Barely had we digested our grades than Mr. Black was handing out the cow-bird quote, as enigmatic as Greek, our reactions due next week—and there'd be one paper a week after that, four in all, a month of Everests to climb.

"What does this quote *mean?*" groaned Beth behind me.

"I guess you'll have to get to the library," said Mr. Black, appearing from nowhere to place his elbows on her desk, his grinning face inches from hers.

I felt suddenly nauseated, clammy with expectation and worry. Receiving an *A+* meant only that I'd have to stage a repeat performance; that was the fate Mr. Black had condemned me to.

Most of my classmates were griping about the red-inked comments on their papers, whispering under their breath, discontent spreading like a virus. My paper had no comments, nothing but the bald grade in a big circle. Dumbly, I read the cow-bird quote over and over. What was it about? Where did I need to begin to unravel it? What if this was the assignment I couldn't crack?

Beth kicked the back of my chair. "I gotta get out of

this class," she whispered. Her reaction paper was facedown on her desk; her face was ashen.

How I missed the easy camaraderie of English, the anonymity of math, even the collective discomfort of science. The last time I'd felt this conspicuously alone and out of synch had been at Beth's party, when no one asked me to dance.

Beth followed through on her threat: within a day she'd made an appointment with Mrs. Eisen, and together they changed her schedule, removing her from Mr. Black's clutches and placing her out of harm's way in a quiet track 2 cit. ed. class.

I missed her, but I still had Alice, Denise, and Anna along for the ride. Who would decipher the cow-bird quote first?

MARCH 11:

I had such a great feeling today. I interpreted the quote finally and have all my information! Eddie likes me. Alice, I luv her! Did good on cit. ed. quiz. I hope I get at least a B- *in science or honor society is out the window. Please, Miss Delray.*

I didn't have to sit with vacillating feelings of failure too long: three days later, we received our penultimate report cards, and I received an *A+* in cit. ed., the third person in

Mr. Black's personal pantheon of remarkable students ever to do so, a fact he announced during class.

On my way out of school that day, I ran into him. I loved seeing teachers when they weren't teaching, when they put down their chalk and grading pens and put on the mask of being an everyday adult, just like my parents or my friends' parents.

"How's your report card?" he asked. Thrilled, I produced it from my book bag and handed it to him, aware as I did that this was the perfect moment, one I likened to standing astride the playground seesaw with one leg on each side, my body balanced perfectly in the middle, the board parallel to the ground.

Stony-faced, he read my grades, pushing his hat back on his head, allowing himself a slight smile. He'd become my at-school father, I realized, more attuned to what interested me than my dad at home. It wasn't that I felt estranged from my father, but I was turning to him less and less for help with school. As science and math became slowly but steadily more peripheral, our evening study sessions dwindled. When it came to English and cit. ed., I knew not only that my father wasn't interested but that he was more or less out of his depth.

Returning my report card, Mr. Black began to talk to me as he'd never done before, words I transcribed that night into my diary: "He was saying what a gr8 all around person I am, he wishes his daughters were like me, and he's saying I'll be happy in life cause of my attitude, etc. I shore hope so!"

Easier, in my diary, to be upbeat and write about how his exhortation pleased me than report what really happened: how, the moment he began speaking, something in me imperceptibly shifted, the seesaw tipped, the equipoise shattered. What insane, invidious species of praise was this, doled out expertly by the men in my life, Mr. Black and my father, which poisoned as it pleased, sounded like honey but hurt like a burn, which soothed and provoked, which I craved and rejected, which made me love and hate myself in equal measure?

How could I have begun, on the tiny page allotted to that day's events, to plumb this morass of untouchable feelings? How could I not think about Mr. Black's own daughters, my classmates, my sister? Why was my achievement trumpeted at their expense? Where would they sit, if there was room at the top for only one?

But this wasn't the worst of it. As Mr. Black placed his briefcase on the floor and rested his foot on top of it, as he continued to laud me, I knew that we were talking now not about my achievement but about his. This segue, this seamless border crossing between his ego and mine, this blurring of his hopes with my own, repulsed me as much as if he had groped for me or stuck his tongue into my mouth. He had intruded upon me, bringing into the conversation his own unmet needs and frustrated expectations, his dissatisfactions with his own life and wife and children. I became the woman he didn't marry, the daughter he didn't bear.

This was praise's dark side—a log in the woods under

which thousands of tiny albino insects swarmed. Absorbing his praise, my father's, I first dissolved and then hardened into something else, less an autonomous breathing person than a cause, a symbol, an exemplar, an athlete whom everyone wants to touch. In me they saw a girl who so far had escaped the traps set for girls and women; somehow I melded the pliable feminine and ambitious masculine in a way that tantalized rather than threatened.

Spooked and sickened, I wanted out of the building, out of my own skin. Keep it to yourself! I wanted to shout at Mr. Black, who showed no signs of shutting up. It was bad enough I'd have to go home and offer my report card to my parents for inspection. Every act of praise seemed one of theft, and I felt thoroughly ripped off.

Oh, I was sick of teachers. I felt pent up, stoppered, detained against my will, kept indoors while around us the world burst into glorious bloom; and I felt betrayed, by my father, Mr. Black, and my own body.

Mutiny must have been in the air or perhaps in the food, for the uprising—the first of several my classmates would go on to stage, locally and nationally, over the course of the next decade—had its roots in the cafeteria.

It began as a joke, a half-baked muscle-flexing scheme with no hope of success. For some reason, Rod's table and ours suddenly decided one day that the food served in the cafeteria was inedible. We joined forces to hatch the plot and spread the word: "Don't buy lunch tomorrow. Brown-bag it."

The boycott had no personal meaning for me; I always brown-bagged it. Day after day, ever since elementary school, I dutifully unwrapped the waxed-paper packets my mother made fresh each morning—tuna fish, cream cheese and jelly, once in a glorious while salami. What appealed to me was our potential to create change, to turn expectation upside down, to wreak even moderate havoc.

The next morning, the air in every homeroom crackled with energy. By the time we got to the cafeteria we could barely control ourselves. Sure enough, only a few stragglers—outcasts so distant from the social current that word had never reached them—left their tables to pick up trays and silverware.

None of us could eat. We played with our brown bags, rustled our aluminum foil. The snooded cafeteria workers, who for as long as we had known them doled out food in a robotic haze, came abruptly to life. They huddled with the cashiers, with the teachers on duty. Suddenly the dean appeared in our midst, and with him Mr. Black in his capacity as adviser to the student council.

These nonplussed adults stood in the center of the room, furiously trying to piece together what was happening. We saw shock and incredulity register on their faces when they realized the scope of what we had pulled off. At one point the ringleaders were asked to identify themselves, and Mr. Black nearly fainted when I approached with a few others.

"A boycott in the cafeteria was staged the other day,"

ran Beth's article in the school newspaper, "to protest unfair and illogical procedures in the lunchroom. The teachers in charge, however, interpreted this action as a boycott of the food itself. This was not what had been intended. At a meeting, members of the class avoided griping about the lunchroom situation, but, instead, offered constructive suggestions on how the situation could be improved."

The meeting she referred to took place after school in the student council/chorus room. It was odd having just five of us assemble in that room which usually held so many. Mr. Black stood at the podium, his foot on a chair, gnawing his thumb. "I don't understand it," he sputtered. "Why couldn't you have voiced your complaints before taking such an irresponsible action as that? And you"—here he turned to me, a superfluous gesture, for I knew he'd been talking almost exclusively to me the entire time, stung by my betrayal, not understanding it as a reaction to his own—"you are one of the most influential people in the entire grade. In the school. Now people are calling you a troublemaker."

In the past, his words would have pierced me; I'd have been choking back my tears. But something had taken possession of me. There I sat, grinning like a maniac, shucking the aura of responsibility and prudence that he'd conferred on me. Fuck you, I would have said if I'd had those words. Just fuck you all.

The next day, Mr. Black sprang a surprise quiz—punishing, I was quite sure, the entire class for my transgression. I got a 60. He handed my paper back to me without a word. Gleefully, I found myself not caring. In fact, I was having the time of my life.

MARCH 29:

The greatest thing happened! I decided to run for class officer. Beth is my campaign manager. I told Eddie and he sounded real real happy and then he shook my hand. In science I opened the door to leave and he came and held it open and said, "After you, Madam!" I was so happy! I got a 10 on the quiz in science and also answered several questions. I need an A!

Success had gone to my head. "Ringleader," "troublemaker"—these were epithets I never thought would apply to me. Yet they fit as well and thrilled me as much as a new party dress.

My decision to run for office had the weight of inevitability: this, I realized, was what Mr. Black had been covertly grooming me for all year. In ninth grade our pedagogic relationship would be severed unless I managed to position myself on the executive board of the student council. Through meetings and memos, we could work together closely, and I'd be able to continue receiving his regularly administered injections of praise.

For I still needed him. His unswerving belief in me was sustenance on which I'd come to depend. Our private conversation in the deserted hallway had been but an aberrant moment in an otherwise long-standing, mutually beneficial affiliation—a moment that, if he'd not long since forgotten it, he would never refer to, would perhaps even deny. He'd been in a kind of trance, I told myself, so entirely had he dropped his guard, revealed his innermost thoughts. He didn't know what he was saying—or else he trusted that I could receive whatever he said as stolidly as an inert gas, slow to react no matter how high the temperature rose. If I jumped to unpleasant conclusions, I'd betray his trust. It was also possible that I'd misinterpreted, or overreacted. I often took things too much to heart. Mr. Black hadn't meant to offend me. And the intentions of others—not my own responses, my parents had taught me—were what counted.

Eddie, president of the eighth-grade class, was seeking reelection, and I wasn't about to oppose him. "Run for vice-president," Mr. Black advised, but that position scared me—too much responsibility. At the same time, the idea of taking minutes was much too demeaning. Only treasurer remained, an office for which I wasn't particularly suited.

But neither was Paula Kaplan, the soft-spoken girl from my math class who decided to run against me. Despite her large track 2 constituency, I smugly assumed I could beat her. To win, I'd simply have to make some campaign posters and deliver a speech in front of a full-school assembly.

The next day, however, Rod stunned me by announcing his candidacy for treasurer. I considered dropping out of the race. After all, math was his best subject. He could manipulate numbers magically in his head, draw up budgets, and balance books, while I filled pages with false starts and erasures. He was also bold and unafraid of spending money, where I was cautious and miserly. By rights, the job should have been his.

On the other hand, I knew that he didn't care about the office the way I did. Whatever motivated him to run—and what it was I couldn't imagine—had nothing to do with wanting to make a contribution to the school. "Nothing personal," he would have said if I had asked him why he'd decided to run against me—not that I did.

I asked virtually no questions, even of myself. The reasons I wanted the job were beyond my ability to articulate at the time: I wanted desperately to give a speech in front of an assembly; I wanted the same kind of visibility I had in cit. ed.; I wanted to return to the school, years in the future, with my husband and children, and find, as we strolled down the hall near the main office, a plaque inscribed with my name as concrete evidence that I had walked these halls, that I'd had an impact. Immortality, the type poets wrote about, was what I was after.

Campaigns for public office, even unsuccessful ones, were infused with an admirable nobility; this I'd learned tracking Goldwater's failed attempt. My friends and I could mount a noble campaign. With their support, I'd take on the school the way I'd taken on Mr. Black's class.

So even though Rod's entry into the race necessitated a primary election, even though I knew in my gut that I wasn't qualified, I didn't withdraw my name. It was as if I finally stepped up to the plate of the fantasy baseball game I'd played in my head years before. This was the big leagues for me, the moment of truth. Heady with the successes of the year, I finally felt ready to take my swing. Exactly one year after my family had moved to Long Island, I proudly threw my hat in the ring and kept it there.

SPRING

April 2:

I had such a damn great time! The play was as dirty as all hell. But it was a panic. Rod is real nice. Alice and Denise are hysterical. Bus ride was fab—boys were drips.

Eight eighth-grade honors English students—four boys and four girls—were handpicked to accompany our ninth-grade counterparts on a field trip to Princeton University to see a performance of *The Birds* by Aristophanes.

The question of whom Mrs. Johnson would select as emissaries had us all in a frenzy for several weeks. That I would go seemed assured—my *Moby Dick* report had seen to that—but I was concerned that Beth, Alice, and Denise be chosen as well, as they were. Rod and Eddie were also selected, for their brains, we assumed. Tom went as the grade's budding journalist, and Steve, the criterion for whose selection escaped us all, rounded out the boys' contingent. There we were, the octagonal nucleus of our English class rounded up for a singular honor.

Snow had hovered in the forecast all week, and we went to bed on the eve of the trip unsure if we'd make it. When I awoke the next morning to icy cold but dry and clear darkness, I nearly wept with relief. I slipped into my best formal clothes—a pale-blue tweed wool suit, a white blouse, a pin affixed to my lapel, nylons, and pumps. Though I normally walked to school, my father insisted on driving me this morning, since I had to be there an hour earlier than usual. Together we ate breakfast in the cold kitchen, desolate as a ghost town without my mother's bustling about. "Ready?" he asked, gulping down the last of his coffee. I envied him his hot drink. Soundlessly he guided the car out of the garage and through the sleepy neighborhood streets, the engine barely purring, neither accelerating nor slowing down except when we arrived at school.

A charter bus, motor running, slightly listing, idled in the school parking lot like a lone, snorting behemoth. My father wanted to stay with me until we boarded, but when he saw the other fathers drop off their children, some not even getting out of their cars to say good-bye, he kissed me and drove off to work—slowly, glancing in the rearview mirror as he cruised out of the development, toward the expressway.

One by one all my friends arrived, the eight of us huddling together as we waited for the intimidating ninth graders and their teachers, sharing without speaking the delicious tang of anticipation. This trip was like a providential rip in the fabric of everyday life; it released us from the cursed daily routine that boxed us in, threatened to break our backs and dampen our spirits.

In the freezing morning, we jumped up and down to keep warm, giddy with excitement, our breath turning to smoke before it vanished. The alluring adult world wafted toward us, a world as improbable as a serendipitous tropical breeze from a paradise we couldn't even imagine, teasing us with all the pleasures it promised if we could only wait a little bit longer. Free for the day! On a field trip, out of school—no parents!

And barely any chaperones. For as the infinitely older and more worldly ninth graders began to assemble, we stumbled on a hidden fringe benefit of being so outclassed and outnumbered: no one knew us. We were as incorporeal as ghosts, beneath notice, a tiny clutch of isolated travelers speaking a foreign language. Grateful for our invisibility, we settled into our seats for the long ride to New Jersey, only to be forgotten about almost entirely.

At the university, we ate lunch somewhere and then were shepherded into a huge auditorium for the play. We sat to the side and in the back; fortunately for us, everything about the production, from costumes and gestures to scenery, codpieces, and phalluses, was much, much larger than life. What began as tittering chuckles soon erupted into waves of ribald laughter as the characters strutted onstage, talking of cloud-cuckoo-land. The stinging political satire came through as clearly as the bawdiness.

Our chaperones squirmed in their seats, anticipating, I think, the flurry of phone calls from concerned parents that would greet them upon our return. Hadn't anyone told them what this play was about? Their utter confusion reaffirmed our deepest suspicions: adults were really overgrown kids. They played at policing us because they were expected to, but in truth they were as much in the dark as we were.

On the bus going home, my girlfriends and I sat together in silent sorority. As a small delegation from our class to the outside world, we felt the bonds between us solidify that day. We had been selected, we knew, because we would most appreciate the opportunity—as well we had. Tomorrow, in class, Mrs. Johnson would ask us to describe the trip and recap the play for our classmates, and each of us knew that despite our best intentions, we weren't up to the task. Our descriptions would be short, inadequate, and flat. None of us had the words to express what we had seen and all we had learned: not simply the play and the teachers' reactions to it, but the limitless green freedom of college: no disruptive bells ringing every forty-five minutes, no hall monitors, no enforced studying. In fact, higher education seemed to take place outdoors, between ivy-covered buildings, in the midst of spires and church bells, whenever you wanted it to.

Like a genie from the lamp, English escaped from its confines that day, from the four walls of our class, from the squat, self-contained building surrounded by sprawling fields. I'd appropriated it—along with Mrs. Johnson, and every book and poem she'd had us read—and woven it into my life. If it were only a boy, we'd be going steady.

April 6:

I started with 18 and now I got 125 signatures! I hope I make it! What if Mrs. Cooper doesn't sign it? Today Eddie

> *signed my petition. He said he was sorry cause he already signed Rod's, but then he crossed his name out there and signed mine. He sounded really sorry too. Mr. Black even told me today that he hopes I win!*

In cit. ed., too, my sights transcended the subject matter and even Mr. Black. Though I wrote four more reaction papers, took numerous surprise quizzes, and read dizzying amounts of text, I was done with all that. I'd aced all I'd had to, made my mark, distinguished myself. For the first time, academic work was pushed to the sidelines, flattened in importance by the steamroller of election fever. Running for office became cit. ed. class in action, as if the campaign journal I'd compiled months before had sprung to vigorous life. Once elected, I'd be placed in the best class of all, an honors class—just me and the other officers and Mr. Black, who'd meet weekly, before the regular student council.

Running a campaign gobbled up most of my time and concentration. The first step was finding enough people to sign my qualifying petition, and then preparation for the three-way primary election.

My house emerged as campaign headquarters: Two or three friends would come home with me each day after school. First we'd have a snack in the kitchen—Mallomars and potato chips and milk, salt alternating with sweet—under my mother's watchful eye. Then we'd retreat to my room, where we'd scour magazines for pictures we could clip, paste on oak tag, and cleverly caption: "Don't miss the boat," we'd write, the pungent ink-black Magic Marker squeaking as we carefully formed the letters. "Vote for Roberta." My name, we quickly realized, eluded easy rhymes.

Already the corridors at school were wallpapered with election posters, but we always managed to find a space in which to squeeze a new one. I didn't stumble over the self-promotion. If anything, the activity of exhorting classmates to vote for me made me feel remote, as if I were someone whose name I recognized but otherwise didn't know that well. To whom would I appeal? Where was my core constituency? Would Paula and I split the girl vote, leaving all the boys to vote for Rod? Or would Rod and I fragment the track 1 vote, leaving everyone else to support Paula? Would allegiance to a candidate come down to gender or to intelligence? Or had I simply emerged as the spokesperson for our circle of friends, those of us who felt disenfranchised, who valiantly tried to straddle the middle ground, neither outcasts nor popularity queens, whose brains outstripped our looks, whose energy and ambition branded us?

APRIL 30:

The greatest day! I WON the primary! I did, honestly. I did, I was so happy, it was told in council, the very last thing! Rod is my opponent. He came over and shook my hand and said Congrats, sounded real good. Paula was cry-

ing—but I was too—even though Rod told me not to. Now comes all important speech before an assembly. So scared! Made Honor Society too! May is such a great month, so much: primary, honors. I hope we didn't make a spectacle of ourselves today. Beth said we might have lost some votes, but Anna thinks it was normal. Hope so! It's gonna be tuff. I love Rod.

Mr. Black made us sit through an entire student council meeting before announcing the primary results. Beth, Anna, and Alice sat with me, even though they weren't class representatives. When the names of the winners were read, mine among them, we shrieked and hugged each other, making a "spectacle" of ourselves, which meant that we showed genuine emotion in public rather than in the privacy of our bedrooms.

Paula, for her part, sat crying quietly, surrounded by her supporters, the perfect, noble gentlewoman, reacting within the bounds of what was expected and revealing only as much muted emotion as other people could comfortably handle. I approached her and we shook hands, then hugged, almost as if she were comforting me. Her soft flesh and downy cheek reminded me of my grandmother's, and brushing against her, I felt very masculine.

I didn't wish to be in her shoes; still, the sight of her acquiescent and ruined face haunted me. Serene, queenly, she sat surrounded by her minions of friends, who murmured to her like a hundred mothers consoling an abject little girl who'd lost her favorite doll, a wordless, maternal language of comfort and caring I couldn't understand, could barely hear.

But what did dignity matter? I'd won. Suddenly I realized how much work was ahead of me: a new slew of posters had to be made, a speech had to be written, and a speech-giving outfit planned. With Paula out of the way, Rod and I were alone in the ring—opponents who were also oddly united. The election enabled us to be yoked together in public as my private feelings had never allowed.

Of all my triumphs in cit. ed., none were necessarily exclusive: my *A+*'s didn't preclude anyone else from achieving the same grade. But my election had caused Paula's defeat—an airtight, unalterable equation.

MATH

Obsessively computing averages—my own and my friends'—to a tenth of a point, in each class, for each marking period, with an eye toward final report cards: this was the most passionate use to which I had put math throughout the year. My diary is peppered with numbers: 86 on this test, 93 on that lab, no surprise quiz too insignificant to remain unrecorded. The difference between earning first honors—a 95 average and higher—and second honors, which ranged from 90 to 95, could hinge on how thoroughly you answered the questions at the end of the chapter that the teacher impulsively assigned in a last-ditch attempt to keep the class quiet. In the end, it all came down to numbers.

That math had other, practical uses we were always reminded, promised, the way a suitor pledges fidelity. Think about having to grocery shop, math teachers would tell us, evoking a mythical time when we'd ascend to adulthood: you'll need to know how to add and subtract, and calculate unit value. And to furnish a house? Purchase a rug? Math is essential.

I thought of math as science's handmaiden, something

not particularly interesting on its own but necessary for all that was interesting. This I knew from my father, whose engineer's respect and admiration for math stopped just short of love. Whatever carpentry project he was in the midst of, he was always knee-deep in math, retrieving his slide rule or yardstick or, best of all, the retractable metal measuring tape with a hook you snagged on the end of a table or piece of lumber before it snapped back to its case like an obedient dog.

Yet the true mathematician in our family, the one who loved numbers for their own sake, was my mother. She'd studied accounting in City College and worked in the bursar's office after graduation until she'd become pregnant with me, retiring then to keep the financial records of our family, write the checks, deal with banks and mortgages, and disburse cash.

"Why didn't you ever take the CPA exam?" I asked her on many occasions, as did my husband, her friends, and the accountants who employed her and came to rely on her precision, her limitless respect for detail, her relentless pursuit of small sums lost while computing bank reconciliations.

She always shrugged and made a gesture with her hand as if to say, "Go on," before saying aloud, "I didn't have the head for it."

But of course she did; in fact, she had both head and heart. She loved numbers, loved their orderliness, their definitiveness, their indisputability.

As a girl I caught this. Even before I could write, I used

to love to sit at my grandmother's rolltop desk, scribbling indecipherable figures on ledger paper and filing them in various pigeonholes. Though I most wanted to be a hairdresser, the thought of sitting at a desk in an office, copying numbers from one page to another with a fat fountain pen, had its attraction. I also loved my miniature black cash register, just like the one Mr. Gulco used in his Bronx appetizing store. After slicing the lox and whitefish just the way my grandfather demanded, he'd remove a thick, stubby pencil from behind his ear, sharpen it with a knife, lick the squared-off tip, and transcribe the numbers from his head onto the side of a brown paper bag, the lead oily and black. Then he added up how much was owed, not one column at a time, as we were taught in school, but in a single gulp.

Yet that morning when my mother and I met with Mrs. Eisen to revamp my schedule in light of school records that had just arrived from Queens, and Mrs. Eisen had mused, "How about we keep you in track 2 math?" my mother didn't object. Neither did I. Would my father have spoken up to question Mrs. Eisen's decision had he been there? Would he have asked, point-blank, if her decision had more to do with scheduling than with math ability?

Look at the record, he would have said. My grades in math were high—not as high as in English and social studies, perhaps, but above 90 each semester. Even in seventh-grade math, despite the fact that I'd missed the last two weeks of school with the chicken pox, I'd come back on the day of the math final to score a 97. "I wish all of my students could contract the chicken pox in June if they'd all perform as well as you did," my seventh-grade math teacher wrote in my autograph book.

I remember his kindness more than his face. Math was an invisible, teacherless subject. The concepts were taught—fractions, decimals—practiced, committed to memory, and tested, each new unit erasing the previous one as effectively as an eraser on the blackboard. The most amazing fact about math was that my seventh-grade math teacher in Queens had the name of a city, Mr. Tulsa.

What led the laconic Mr. Tulsa, who in private must have fancied himself a drill sergeant, to pick up a piece of chalk in front of a room of twelve-year-olds I can't imagine. He was the least nurturing teacher I'd ever had. All business, he subscribed to the pedagogic technique according to which teachers refrain from showing any emotion save annoyance for the first three months of class, so that the first halfhearted smile, indulged in just before Christmas vacation, becomes an occasion for rejoicing. I didn't warm to him—I wasn't supposed to, I realize now.

Only one incident stands out in my mind: In the middle of a lesson on a bleak Friday in November, the classroom phone rang. Mr. Tulsa picked it up, stood silent for a moment, and then shooed us back to our homeroom. "What is it, what happened? Why are we leaving in the middle of a lesson?" We besieged him with questions, but the longer we loitered, the angrier he became. "Get out of here, get to homeroom!" he yelled at us, white as chalk, leaving it to our homeroom teacher to tell us that President Kennedy had been shot in Dallas.

His behavior—not telling us what he so clearly knew—puzzled me even then. But what thoroughly rankled me was his lack of notice. "He never calls on me!" I wrote in my diary on several occasions. I'd never had this experience before. I wasn't the type to wildly raise my hand at every question, nor was I excessively shy. In general, I volunteered when I was pretty sure I knew the answer, and was used to being acknowledged with some regularity. Mr. Tulsa thwarted me, broke the pattern, played havoc with my expectations.

> Finally *called on in math, but gave 78% instead of* 78.00%, *which of course was wrong!!*

I hated him for being so finicky; we all did. Numbers have no mercy, he never hesitated to tell us. If it's not completely right, if even the tiniest decimal is misplaced or missing, if the answer is in the least incomplete, it's all wrong. Nothing personal.

But everything about school had been personal to me. In the face of his mercilessness, I turned to my father for help and support. Almost every night after dinner, I'd approach him moments after he picked up the newspaper, and I'd whine, "I need help with this stupid math." How he must have sighed inwardly, but he never turned me down, never told me to wait. He simply read the problem, borrowed my pencil, and set about figuring out the solution using techniques he'd learned years before, in grammar school. For a few minutes I'd savor our collaboration; like coconspirators, we sat in our own bubble, while elsewhere in the house my mother and sister cleaned up from dinner, colored, got ready for bed—daily, benighted, dreary household activities that never intersected with the abstract and esoteric.

"But that's not the way Mr. Tulsa told us to solve it!" I'd suddenly burst out when my father's calculations took him down a path I couldn't follow, making him defend the validity of his approach. That there was more than one way to approach a problem didn't intrigue but rather angered and scared me. Lacking an intuitive feel for math, for numbers, I had to pin all my hopes on learning the rules and their rigorous, inflexible application.

Desperately, I'd try to retrace the steps toward the solution Mr. Tulsa had written on the blackboard. Although I could follow the steps well enough in class, at home I felt entirely lost. Where should I start? What was the first variable? Which formula to use? My father and I would argue. Sometimes I'd cry; often he'd become exasperated. Mutual annoyance hung between us as it never did in the playground.

I wanted to succeed, to master this intractable, elusive subject. Impassive, abrupt, and self-involved as he was, standing back to admire his equations like an artist before his canvas, Mr. Tulsa somehow managed to communicate that math had meaning for him, that he appreciated its elegance, that he relied on its certainty as you do an old friend who has never let you down—and that we should too.

This year, though, I had Mrs. Villard, who had no discernible relationship to math. I came to think of her class as an intermission, time out from the high drama of every other class, particularly English and cit. ed., a respite from my friends madly competing with each other in track 1 math—in short, as an exile.

Was every track 2 class like this? Is that what "average" students were served up, a bland, mechanistic presentation of facts and figures to be memorized and spit back on quizzes and tests? Were track 2 students the "girls" of the school system, branded with unshakably low expectations? Imagine if English class consisted of nothing more than sentence parsing; if, instead of packing a year's worth of grammar lessons into a deadly two-week unit, the entire year, forty-five minutes a day, were devoted to sniffing out verbs and nouns.

Not until college would I come face-to-face with a math teacher who roundly dismissed the notion that math and girls didn't mix. Dr. Henley, who chaired the department, was a shy, kindly man with wispy hair, wire-rimmed glasses, and skin so delicately alabaster his nose turned red from the sun during a walk from his office to the classroom. No matter what the temperature, he wore a short-sleeved shirt, loose pieces of chalk stored in its pocket. I registered for his section of introductory calculus only because my boyfriend dared me to; I, in turn, dared him to sign up for metaphysical poets.

On Dr. Henley's first test I received a 65; on the second, a 60. Each time, I had the familiar feeling that I understood the material, that I could solve the problem at hand using a previous one as a model. But problems never exactly repeated themselves; each new one came with its own complications, and I always felt like Gretel in the forest after the birds had eaten her brother's carefully strewn bread crumbs.

"I think I should drop the class," I told Dr. Henley during his late-afternoon office hours, fully prepared to cry. (My boyfriend had long since dropped poetry.) His office was as messy as my mother's desk was impeccable, and he leaned toward me with such concern in his barely blue eyes that I saw at once that I needn't resort to tears.

"Don't do that," he said, reaching for his roll book to see my grades.

"I'm trying just about as hard as I can," I said. "Maybe I should take it pass/fail."

"That may be useful," he mused. "I don't think you'll fail. How can I make things clearer for you?"

He gave me a minilesson, and I left his office confident that I'd do better on the next test. Only I didn't; my grades hovered around 65. He graciously gave me a P even though I failed the final.

To him, math was poetry, numbers and formulas as pliable as words, as lilting as melodies; it whispered of mysteries and had its own buried beauty and elegance, the kind that revealed itself the more you looked. But his influence came too late. For me, math remained the subject I was always on the verge of understanding, the one I appreciated much more from a distance than up close.

Twenty-two years later, my son scores high on his math aptitude test and is placed in accelerated math. Last year math came easily, effortlessly; this year, he's struggling. I hear him slam his book, break his pencil. "I hate math," he announces. "It's the worst. It's stupid and useless and I hate it."

"Come on the bed with me," I say from where I sit reading the newspaper, looking forward to the crossword puzzle. He shows me the problem—some kind of equation. Miraculously, a memory trace arises in a cortical crevice, the way a cluster of goose bumps appears and vanishes on your skin.

"I think this is what you do," I say, taking the pencil from Ben. I remember what to do. It's pleasant, almost as pleasing as a crossword puzzle. I proceed one step at a time, the way my father always told me. I'm actually enjoying myself.

"But that's not the way Mrs. Gerry told us to do it," my son whines, wresting the pencil from me. I tell him it needs sharpening, that he needs an eraser, that he needs to take more space for marginal calculations, that he should do everything on paper, nothing in his head. He keeps at his smudged numbers, always arriving at the wrong answer.

"It's stupid and I hate it." He throws his book across the bed, behavior my father would never have tolerated. "I hate having to be so exact. I'm much better at being general."

We're both more comfortable with words and images, my son and I. We like to manipulate and insinuate, to explain and cajole. I feel my own anxiety surfacing, as fresh and potent as if I were back in eighth grade and Mrs. Eisen is explaining to me that I received such low scores on the spatial and mathematical reasoning subtests of the recently administered aptitude battery that she's positive it's a mistake. Should I tell him I hated math too—that it was the one subject I couldn't master by willpower alone, that it remained out of my grasp? Or should I exhort him to remain open to it, not to discard it, as I had? To stay in the accelerated program so he'd get the better teachers?

I'm terrified that he has the same wired-in response to math that I do. Add numbers in my head? Figure out whether the pound or two-pound jar of spaghetti sauce is a better buy? My muscles clamp, my brain clouds, I have a mini panic attack. Numbers and operations no sooner flash through my mind than they evanesce. I can't stammer an answer. After all the figuring and calculations, the narrow line where the answer should appear never fails to make me feel flustered and short of breath.

None of my girlfriends, even those who stayed in track

1 math through high school, pursued careers that involve math. For those who became doctors and psychologists, statistics remained the most dreaded course, the Everest of their professional training. And every time I contemplated pursuing a career in science, even to the point where I requested applications from medical schools, the prospect of having to take statistics stopped me cold.

Then, a few years ago, Game Boy entered my life, as a Chanukah present for Ben. A palm-sized, handheld video game system not much bigger than a soft gray paperback, it resembled an old-fashioned transistor radio and was just about as intimidating. You even held it between two hands, as if you were reading.

Tetris, the Russian game that was packaged with the system, wasn't like any video game I'd ever seen. No sooner did Ben insert the cartridge than strains of haunting electronic balalaika music filled his bedroom. Its visuals also differed dramatically from the standard-issue blood-and-gore graphics, I noticed, playing novitiate to Ben's master. He was a patient but old-fashioned teacher, eschewing hands-on learning, refusing to relinquish Game Boy once during my entire hour-long lesson.

Instead, I watched over his shoulder as he simultaneously played and supplied the play-by-play. At the top center of the miniature screen, an L-shaped object appeared and then slowly, with almost balletic poise, began to fall. One button rotated the object on its axis; another moved it right to left. Then another object appeared, this one a square. The goal, it seemed, was to manipulate each of six differently shaped pieces midair and deposit them, on the bottom of the screen, in neat horizontal rows.

Simple enough, it seemed—at least until Ben fell asleep and I spirited the game into bed with me later that night. Then I struggled to figure out how to start the contraption, how to turn off the music, what each of the buttons did. When I managed to lift my eyes from the screen, I was shocked to realize that nearly two hours had passed, that I was as sweaty as I'd be after an aerobic workout, and that I'd managed to construct a brave ten lines.

"Very good," Ben told me next morning in his most condescending tone. His record, however, was ninety-nine lines. And a woman I met at the school-bus stop told me she routinely topped one hundred twenty. I was incredulous. My competitive spirit, long dormant, came out swinging. A Tetris disability was not something I would take in stride.

Each night after the kids were in bed, Game Boy and I had a date. I'd click it on, my thumbs itching as soon as I heard Nintendo's irrepressible two-toned musical trademark. Slowly, I'd begin playing, the shapes tumbling so languorously I could manipulate them just for the hell of it, in a gratuitous display of prowess, with plenty of time to position them just right. Gradually, almost imperceptibly, they'd begin raining down with slightly more urgency. I'd bring the game in closer, my arms tucked near my waist, and squint down at the green-gray screen. I'd push the buttons a bit more forcefully, with more determination, manipulating the game this way and that, grimacing and groaning, cradling, almost caressing the toy. Soon I'd be importunate, begging the genie of the game to conjure up certain shapes—the square, or the skinny rectangle, to insert on the side, just there, completing four lines at once. A tetris! A faint sheen of sweat would appear on my upper lip; my breathing would quicken. Just one more line and I'd get another tetris, one more shape in the right place; it's moving faster now, so fast I can hardly keep up; one more; can't stop. . . .

Within a week, I stumbled over two startling discoveries: the more I played, the better I became; and I wanted to play all the time. "Just one more game," I promised myself, twelve-thirty at night, as if I were my own mother, reprimanding me for staying up too late on a school night and squandering my eyesight on foolishness. But no sooner did I hear that humiliating little raspberry indicating another lost game than I had to start anew. I simply couldn't help myself.

In short, I became an addict. Furtively I played at the kitchen table while waiting for the spaghetti water to boil, played while my sons marinated in bubble bath, played while my computer booted up. The rotating shapes appeared in my mind's eye before I went to sleep; on line at the supermarket, I played out entire perfect games in my head.

• • •

"Most girls have trouble in the areas of mathematical and spatial reasoning," Mrs. Eisen had assured my mother, explaining my 13th-percentile scores in these areas. She took this as a final vindication that her decision to keep me out of the eddying shoals of track 1 math had been correct after all.

I remembered those tests as an exercise in free fall. Asked to rotate objects mentally or to unfold and flatten three-dimensional structures, I experienced an initial clarifying moment—a flash, in which my pencil was drawn to the right answer as if I were dowsing for water. Then I reconsidered, a fatal mistake, scrutinizing the other options, until all of them seemed equally plausible.

Yet what was Tetris but timed spatial reasoning? With a little practice and encouragement, I had learned to manipulate objects in my head—to rotate them, make them fit, use the skill I was convinced I had in shortest supply.

MAY 9:

> A Separate Peace *by John Knowles. Remember that—it's one of the best books I ever read. I kept thinking about it all day. It was very impressive. I looked real good today. I rewrote my speech, it's good. I feel very good, I know I did well in science, I feel it in my bones. I love that book!*

The book traveled through our crowd like a relay-race baton: discovered first by Beth, our scout, handed off to Denise and then to me and then to Alice, our usual route. Boys at a WASPy prep school—the characters and setting of *A Separate Peace* couldn't have been more foreign to us. More egregious, it contained not a single female character. Yet so adept and practiced were we at the art of identifying with male protagonists that we hardly even noticed these differences, much less labeling them as obstacles. The book did something for us no other had: it concentrated on a close-knit group of friends, at school, on the cusp of becoming adults.

The plot was simple enough: Gene Forrester, the narrator, is implicated, but only in his own mind and by his closest associates, in the crippling and death of his friend Phineas, an improbably untarnished boy who until prep school has effortlessly and admirably loped through his life.

Did Gene push Phineas out of the tree? This is the question at the book's fulcrum. The answer, which I inferred only after many readings, seemed to be an ambiguous yes. He didn't actually push, he jostled the branch.

But why he wanted, in his heart, to hurt Phinny is the deeper and more sinister question, implicating unfathomable forces within the human soul, something beyond the easy categories of good and evil.

I didn't so much read the book as absorb it through my pores. Like a poem, it had no "meaning" to extract surgically and carry around; the lesson inhered in the story and, like a time-release capsule, allowed me, upon each successive reading, to probe more deeply into the book's dark heart. Did Phineas forgive Gene? Did Gene forgive himself? From my extended conversation with the book, I could guess at the answers but couldn't articulate them: my vocabulary wasn't supple enough.

Significantly, all these conscience-riddled questions are posed against the backdrop of World War II. Unlike the other wartime novels we'd read, in *A Separate Peace* the hostilities unfolded offstage, with the sound turned way down—no thundering guns, no brutality. I suppose this is what renders the book a "young adult" novel: the certainty that one's own little drama is more important than what happens out on the battlefield or at the peace table.

Yet this is precisely what spoke to me. In other books, the interior drama was swept away, often thoroughly overwhelmed by the flow of history. But what determines this flowing tide, what dooms us to fight each other, is the inner war, the inner struggle, the inexplicable desire we have to jostle a branch—and our patent inability to explain that desire. I was fast becoming a microcosmologist.

The book accomplished for me what peering through a

microscope at a drop of pond water smeared on a glass slide does for a budding scientist: it revealed an exotic, teeming universe that would otherwise have remained invisible. And just as single-cell water creatures are ground zero of the food chain, without which the rest of life as we know it couldn't exist, so too the forces swirling in the psyche that couldn't be explained or denied, with which one had to broker a "separate" peace, seemed the building blocks of our humanity.

I'd reread Gene's reflection in the book's last paragraph so often that I could recite it as a kind of prayer:

> All of them, all except Phineas, constructed at infinite cost to themselves these Maginot Lines against this enemy they thought they saw across the frontier, this enemy who never attacked that way—if he ever attacked at all; if he was indeed the enemy.

In 1964, only a fool couldn't identify the enemy. The Vietnamese War was in its earliest stages of escalation, and we were all hawks, earnest subscribers to the domino theory, from which we wouldn't be swayed for two more years.

Yet in my personal life the enemy was harder to discern. Was it Mr. Black? Miss Delray? My overprotective, restrictive parents? My jealous friends? Myself? *A Separate Peace* divided the world for me into those with easy answers and those who sensed, as I was beginning to do, that under close inspection most everything gave up its shape and blurred its very borders, and that easy opposites—good and bad, friend and enemy—were Siamese twins, sharing too many vital organs for one to be destroyed without, inadvertently, the other

MAY 11:

Everyone thinks my speech is FAB. I don't know. What the hell is Rod gonna say? I wanna win so bad!!

Back and forth I traveled that spring, crossing the threshold between my inner and outer lives so frequently that I would have worn out a passport.

I knew I'd give a better speech than Rod; when it came to grades in oral presentations in both English and cit. ed., mine put his to shame. He was much more self-conscious than I, and he couldn't seem to lose his smirk or his nervous habit of perpetually touching his hair.

But he seemed unduly confident. Did *he* stand in front of his bedroom mirror, wishing his hair were longer, or shorter, or a different color, or that he had something new to wear? Did he wonder whether or not he'd trip or get booed? I didn't think so. Not for a second.

During lunch a few days before the election, Beth convinced me to rehearse my speech in front of her: she would come home with me after school, sit on my bed, take notes, and offer constructive criticism; I'd use my desk as the podium and practice my gestures.

We took our time leaving, laughing by our lockers, anticipating the vote, feeling the momentum, giddy with how easy it had been to come within spitting distance of victory.

Then we saw it, a few words scrawled in ballpoint pen over one of my carefully composed posters: "Suck her tits." Beth clapped her hand over her mouth; I froze. We stared at it openmouthed, as if trying to decipher the three short words, as if they needed sounding out, neither of us speaking because that would acknowledge the fact that this had happened. If we both stayed quiet, maybe we were both dreaming. "We have to find Mr. Black," she said finally, though neither of us could get our legs to work.

He was in the faculty office, grading papers. We told him we had something to show him downstairs. So little time elapsed from the moment he saw it to the moment he ripped it off the wall and rolled it up that I wondered if he'd even read the offending words. "Go on home," he told us. "I'll take care of this."

Beth and I walked home in virtual silence, the vulgarity of the graffiti in the air between us. I felt as if someone had ripped off my blouse the way Mr. Black ripped off the poster. "Tits"—a word I'd never used in relation to myself. I'd never seen Mr. Black so overwrought. Yet at the same time his spring to action rebuked me. How foolish we were, how naive, to have left the poster on the wall even a fraction of a second longer than we had to.

We should have ripped it down right then. I didn't even know how to protect myself.

"I bet it was Joey Rothstein," Beth said when we reached my house. He was a basketball star who smirked through all the classes we shared and counted himself one of Rod's most vocal supporters.

"Yeah, maybe" I said. But frankly it was easier for me to imagine a total stranger walking into school and scrawling "Suck her tits" across my poster than to think that anyone in the school who knew anything at all about me—even Joey Rothstein—would do such a thing.

The next morning, after the Pledge of Allegiance and the day's announcements, Mr. Black took the microphone in the main office and informed the student body that anyone caught defacing campaign posters would be subject to the harshest disciplinary measures. Even over the scratchy loudspeaker we could tell his voice was hoarse with fury. He mentioned no names, and instantly the room was buzzing: "What happened? What's he talking about?"

On and on he went, threatening to halt elections, to dissolve student council. Enough already, I silently pleaded with him, squirming in my chair. The longer he harangued, the more people would infer that I was the injured party. He hadn't yet realized that there was nothing else to do. We were powerless. What had been done couldn't be erased. Nothing would take those words away, not ever.

• • •

Except time. Of all the incidents I remember from eighth grade, running for office was perhaps the most momentous. Yet I'd completely forgotten about it until I reread my diaries. And buried within the deep folds of this repression squatted another—the graffiti on my campaign poster. Even more shocking was the fact that the original incident merited only a one-sentence P.S. attached to a longer entry.

At the time, it was important that the incident not break my stride, that I proceed with the campaign, deliver my speech. Only after thirty years do I see that these words unleashed a black magic so potent that I didn't even realize I was under its spell until right now. No one asked me how it made me feel. I never asked myself.

But now I'll respond to it, to whoever wrote it, to the entire landscape and climate of that year: Finding my defaced poster was like being walked in on while on the toilet, or watching your clothes blow off, item by item, on a crowded street during a gale intended just for you. It sucked the wind out of me like a punch to the stomach. It left me gasping.

Before, I'd been a marathoner unaware that she had a terrible limp until a heckler on the sidelines called attention to it. I'd only acknowledged my corporeal self when it came to sports; then, I was someone who was coordinated, who could run, hit a ball with a stick or racket, ride a bike. The moment I had to think of myself as someone with tits, I faltered internally. The secret of my success, it seemed, wasn't so much in being a boy as in not being aware of having a body.

No words written on Rod's poster, however, would have skewered him as effectively as I had been—nothing, not even "motherfucker," would have caused him shame. I had no idea how to hide all I had to hide and be out in the world.

Speech day, I woke up thinking of Eleanor Roosevelt. She'd long been my hero—I'd read countless biographies—though I'd forgotten about her in the flood of media attention to Jackie Kennedy.

Of course! How fitting that Eleanor rescue me. For years she'd been the only woman with any political visibility, and though our lives couldn't have been more different, I identified with her totally.

Jackie, on the other hand, though closer in age, remained entirely remote, even before the assassination. In many ways she was my worst nightmare: an intelligent woman, a college girl who'd set out to have a career, she was sideswiped by marriage (even if it was to an up-and-coming, rich, handsome politician), motherhood, and interior design. Redecorating the White House? Walking through historic rooms and talking about drapery? What self-respecting woman with half a brain in her head could carry off that performance with a straight face? The very idea was infuriating.

And after Dallas, even though I grieved with her, my estrangement grew. That she didn't cry—and that every writer covering the story commented on her unshakable reserve—puzzled me so deeply I couldn't even frame the logical question: Who wouldn't cry at her husband's funeral? Why shouldn't you?

Much better to remember big, ungainly Eleanor, who, despite her wealth, heritage, and power, looked like my grandmother. Fitting no premade mold of femininity, she worried about her personal life, her homeliness, her height and girth. She'd probably been told that her feet were too big, that she rolled like a drunken sailor when she walked, that she needed to look like more of a lady.

Crossing the stage from the bank of seats where all the candidates waited to the podium after my name was called, I tried to peer into the audience. My friends, seated with their homerooms, were scattered. How insignificantly small my core constituency was. Day after day, segregated into our track 1 classes, my friends and I seemed numberless. But here, interspersed among the entire student body, with kids from tracks 2 and 3, we were revealed as a tiny current in the ocean of the school. From pockets of the auditorium I heard isolated bursts of applause. Everyone else, the hundreds of students I knew a little bit or not at all, sat relatively quietly and impassively.

"To many of you," I began, reading from my typescript, "the student council is nothing more than a piece of paper entitled 'Minutes.'" I fingered the flower pin on the lapel of my light-blue-and-white tweed suit, hoped my stockings weren't sagging around my ankles, and shifted my weight in my blue pumps. To my audience, I attempted to explain why the student council should play a more central role in their school lives, and then I segued into the various programs and ideas I'd dreamed up: I would establish a yearbook and a literary magazine, distribute student I.D. cards, inaugurate a care-package program, begin a series of special assemblies, place a gripe box and a student bulletin board in the lunchroom. My "final ambition, which I hope will galvanize the entire student body," I said, would be to find a school overseas with whom we could correspond.

After choking back the initial jitters, I actually began to enjoy myself. I liked the way my voice sounded through the filter of my own ears and the scratchy mike, and that I could string words together without being interrupted; that I could block out those who were nodding off and focus on Alice, for I'd found her in the crowd and she was sitting straight up, staring deeply into my eyes, encouraging me to go on, nodding slightly so only I could see. "Yes," she seemed to be saying. "Keep going, for all of us."

"Through my ideas outlined now, great interest and stimulation can be aroused. Together, using the sky as our limit, we can truly aim high. Thank you."

Slightly sweaty, overtaken by a bad case of the shakes—every cell atremble, though outwardly my body betrayed no movement at all—I listened to the applause, more than polite, less than thunderous. Finishing a speech was like returning from a country where they didn't speak the language and the water tasted different. Oddly enough, walking back to my seat, I recalled my *Moby Dick* presentation and its aftermath of exhilaration, how my words had resonated in our drab classroom. Now I felt nothing but drained and let down despite the grand setting, the cadence and words of my speech already forgotten.

Rod spoke next. In the crowd I located Alice again, smiling at me like a proud mama. Rod's speech was short and dry. He didn't fidget as much as I thought he would. He received a good hand as well, and winked at me as he took his seat.

The rest of the day passed strangely. It felt odd to be so dressed up in school, my clothes branding me in the same way bubble-gum corsages pinned to your chest marked you on your birthday. A candidate on election day is granted a curious immunity, suspended in a languorous limbo between the certainties of victory or defeat. No obligations or responsibilities clung to me. For the moment I was curiously exempted, almost royalty.

May 17:

I lost. They told us after school. I lost by 50 votes out of 850. I don't feel too bad cause if I'm chairman of the Elections Committee I'll be on the executive board anyway. But I wanted to win, see my name on that plaque. Eddie won though. I hope he becomes President. Everyone was great to me. I didn't cry though. I want to win, it's bad to lose.

Mr. Black offered me the chairmanship of the election committee as a consolation prize. An earnest suitor, he tried to woo me by stressing the importance of the post: I'd oversee procedures, count petition signatures, certify speeches. He regaled me with tales of all we'd accomplish—the elimination of graffiti on campaign posters, for example. I'd be a member of the executive committee after all. I told him I'd have to think about it.

That afternoon, after the bell, I took the long way out of the building, walking down the corridor leading to the main office, past the plaques listing the officers of the student council for each year. None listed committee chairmen. I felt the sting of certain obscurity, like an actor who'd been offered a job as a stagehand after missing her entrance and garbling her lines.

In no hurry to get home, I walked into the empty auditorium. I often lingered in school, reluctant to leave, school speaking to me of a different self than the one at home. I loved the building when it was empty; I could almost hear it settle, hear reverberating off the lockered walls the shouts and cries and bustle of the just completed day. How inestimably lucky I was to be a walker, without a bus to catch, free to loiter, to amble down deserted hallways and peer into empty classrooms—chairs and desks askew, paper littering the floor, leftover lessons etched on chalkboards. It was a comforting world, a world whose dimensions I fit. How much like a sheltering cave it felt, especially when I remembered the open spaces of Princeton, which promised a freedom so vast I feared it in advance.

I sat in the last row of seats, directly under the projection booth, and stared at the stage. That's where I stood, where I'd delivered my speech. How had I looked from here? How had I sounded? According to Miss Delray, the sound waves put in motion by my speech would travel to the very edge of the universe, perfectly preserved. Were my plans for improving the quality of the student council and enriching the lives of my fellow students pulsing outward, forever indestructible?

When I looked up, Mr. Black was standing in the aisle, his briefcase in hand, looking at me and smiling. I smiled back, and he sat beside me.

"Your speech was very good." I was glad that he didn't continue, that he didn't add that it was better than Rod's. We both knew that.

"You know," he said, putting his arm around the back of my chair, "if you were a boy, you'd have no trouble at all getting into Yale, I'm sure of it."

I smiled at him, because I was in the habit of smiling when he spoke to me, and I knew from the rhythm of his speech and his relaxed body language that he intended a compliment. Yet once again it was a compliment that cut several ways at once. Was it my fault I wasn't a boy? And since I wasn't, where did that leave me: where would I go, where would I fit, to what could I look forward? Wasn't there a girl equivalent of Yale? Was there no remaining option for me? Was it Yale or nothing?

"You'll end up manager of the Yankees"—that's how my father had teased me when baseball was the center of my life. Whenever I brought home an outstanding report card, he said, "You'll be the first woman president." At first these prophecies pleased me; I imagined myself a frontierswoman, shattering gender expectations with a single bound. But all these exhortations to achieve were predicated on my becoming a man. As an ambitious girl, all I knew was what professions I couldn't enter, the colleges I couldn't attend.

Four years later, my father would greet me at the breakfast table, the *New York Times* in his hand, with the wonderful news that in an inadvertent feat of perfect timing, Yale had just decided to admit women—all I had to do was write for an application.

In his jubilation, he didn't notice my dejection. I'd come to think of choosing a college much the same way I thought of clothes shopping: faced with all the possibilities, I couldn't imagine myself anywhere; nor could I imagine why any school would want to accept me over anyone else. Anyway, I knew that every girl in the country whose average topped 95, as mine and all my friends' did, was having this exact conversation with her parents at this very moment.

Because the prospect of explaining to my father and my guidance counselor why I didn't want to apply to Yale required more energy than simply acceding, I sent away for an application and filled it out perfunctorily, as I did all of them. By then I'd realized that perfunctory would do fine. I'd become very adept at calibrating exactly how much effort to expend toward a required end. I'd become aware of the gap that existed between that level and the level on which I had worked in junior high school, when I'd pushed every atom in my body toward a goal. I'd long given that up. It wasn't exactly that I had coasted through high school; it was rather that, like any seasoned performer, I knew how hard I had to work in order to elicit appreciative gasps from my audience—and that achievement at this level fell short of my personal best.

Yale rejected me, as I expected, though one girl from our class was accepted and trundled up to New Haven with Rod. I'd been accepted at another Ivy League school, but instead I packed my bags for the State University of New York at Binghamton, whose squat buildings tucked into scrubby hills reminded me of the schools I'd been attending. It was less a college than an extension of high school. I even roomed with Alice. We fixed up our room to resemble our bedrooms at home and continued the conversation we'd been having for the past five years. Though I'd always envisioned college as an expansion, I burrowed within, hunkered down, read and wrote, bided my time.

"Can I give you a lift home?" Mr. Black asked, unaware of the direction my thoughts had taken. I thanked him and told him I'd walk home; I lived close by.

That night, I decided to take the job of election committee chairman. "Anyway, there'll be other elections," I wrote in my diary. "In a year or two, I'll just try again."

But I never did.

ELECTIVES

To Rutherford, struggling all year to remain alive, stepping into home ec was an act of resuscitation. Seeing Mrs. Cooke, in her frilly bowed blouses or cinched shirtwaist dresses covered by an apron, putter around the room, check the oven, test the iron, thread a needle, brought out the last oppositional vestiges of the boy within me. Gasping for breath after the body blows he'd sustained all year, he shuddered and staggered to life.

With him came a disdainful attitude toward every appliance, utensil, and activity in the room. I never thought Mrs. Cooke noticed, but perhaps she did. Just because she didn't react to our snickers didn't mean that she didn't hear them. Yet she remained unperturbed. Play all you want, girls, at being scholars and academics, at working on your grades, she tacitly told us. You'll end up in the kitchen, just like me.

In Bayside, the pocket of Queens where I lived during the mid and late fifties, it was clear, even to young children, that men had agency and women toiled quietly just beyond the range of vision.

I can't remember how my mother filled her days. Housework wasn't called homemaking or household engineering back then; it wasn't called anything—it had no name. It was simply done, day in, day out. The paradox coiled like a snake at the core of housework was this: the better you did it, the more invisible you became. Preparing for his role in *The Remains of the Day,* Anthony Hopkins remarked that the essence of a good butler is that the room is emptier when he is in it; so too did housewives of the postwar era strive to erase themselves. Food appeared, clothes got worn, washed, ironed, folded, and worn again, but to dwell on these subjects, to think about them, was to think about breathing.

Mothers also stayed put, except when they went to the basement to do the laundry or to the supermarket. On summer afternoons they carried their beach chairs to the park across the street from the apartment building, positioned them in a tight cluster facing the sun, put on their sunglasses, and told us to go play. We saw them next hours later, when the Good Humor and Bungalow Bar trucks cruised down the block, their melodies wafting in the still, humid air. When our mothers went upstairs to prepare dinner, we stayed outside.

None of them drove cars—they didn't need to. In Bayside, schools, stores, doctors, synagogue, and library were within walking distance. The women were as tethered to the development as their mothers and grandmothers had been to their villages in Europe. Yet everything fun, everything adventurous and alluring—the beach, the amusement park, relatives, better playgrounds, better-stocked libraries—was a car ride away. Fathers were our passports out; mothers couldn't get us there.

Except for Ester, a Jewish refugee from Germany, whose driver's license was one more exoticism, like her accent. She drove a two-tone Rambler, a car so much smaller than my father's Chevrolets that it seemed like a toy. One glorious weekday each summer, the men at work, she'd invite my sister, my mother, and me to accompany her and her two daughters on a jaunt to Sunken Meadow Beach. The trip took about an hour but felt like forever. In the back of the car, untethered by seat belts, we four girls would endlessly change places, squatting on the floor, lying across the rear window ledge, sticking feet out of open windows—behavior never tolerated in my father's car. The entire outing had an illicit air, probably because there were no men around. Ester herself was an anomaly I could have studied for hours: she wore skirts but a man's watch; she kept her hair short but had a feminine, infectious laugh. Everything about her defied easy categorization.

"Organization is the key to running a smooth kitchen, girls," Mrs. Cooke would trill, but we put this adage in the trash with all her other admonitions: Never put pins in your mouth, don't taste raw batter, never test the iron by wetting your finger and touching it. As if we hadn't watched our own mothers doing exactly these things for our entire lives.

The first half of the year, we studied cooking, preparing muffins and coleslaw, puddings and casseroles, all tasteless and dry. Cooking interested me not at all, but it was better than sewing, which we began midyear.

The goal of the class—in fact, the climax of the year—was a fashion show for our parents, to be held on the never-used patio in the center of the school. Not only would we learn to walk like models, wearing the dresses we ourselves had sewn, but we'd also cater the event for our appreciative mothers: finger food, punch, cookies. Mrs. Cooke never looked as radiant as when she spoke about the show.

"What are you going to wear to the Honor Society dinner?" Alice asks. We're sitting on her bed. She's thumbing through the new issue of *Seventeen,* stopping every few pages to study a particular outfit. Sometimes she simply frowns and moves on; sometimes she puts her index finger to her lips and slowly shakes her head yes. Then she folds down the corner of the page and turns to the next.

I study the outfits not to see which ones appeal to me—that task is hopelessly beyond me—but to try to predict which pages will catch her eye. I always fail. She zips right by the skirt and sweater combinations I find cute and stops at those I never in a million years would have selected.

In a few days she'll go to a store with her mother and return with a new seasonal wardrobe that will correspond to the clothes in the magazine—a bleeding madras blazer, for example. The stores my parents and I go to for my clothes don't stock anything that resembles an outfit in *Seventeen.*

So I always agree with her. When it comes to clothes, she is the guru and I the novice. In reality, I have no taste of my own. I can't imagine that the girl on the page could be me, that I could find those clothes, put them on, and look like her.

From my family I've inherited a shopping disability, from which I suffer to this day. My parents bought my sister and me well-made clothes, but we never approached a store with a firm knowledge of what we liked and what look we wanted to achieve. Faced with too many possibilities—the rustle and whoosh of fabric, the jangle of belts and click of high heels, all promising something none of us could define—we were virtually paralyzed. If we could be anybody by putting on certain clothes, then how were we to choose whom to be? Invariably we took refuge in something pastel, slightly frilly or nautical, nothing suggestive, and just about everything at least one size too big.

"That's very becoming," my parents would say when I emerged from the fitting room, their best compliment. What it meant was that the clothes were safe, unobtrusive, plain, prim, concealing. Bright colors were out, as was black—too somber for a young girl. By concentrating on sartorial details—an embroidered collar, concealed buttons—we didn't have to focus on the larger issue: how the clothes looked, their shape and cut, whether or not they were flattering or made a statement. I still rely on others—my husband, these days—to help me select what I wear.

"My blue-and-white tweed suit," I tell Alice, the same one I wore to Princeton, the same one in which I delivered my campaign speech. It's not as if I have much choice. The only remaining sartorial decision involves which pin to wear in my lapel.

But no pin helped me feel as if I belonged in the clothes I wore.

The Butterick pattern I selected for the fashion show, a smart, two-piece number composed of a close-fitting sheath and a bolero jacket, seemed sophisticated and flattering. My mother came with me to the Fabric Barn, and together we settled on turquoise for the dress and a floral swirl of turquoise and green for the jacket.

Easy enough. But we also had to buy lining and interfacing, sizing and piping, and dozens of other notions with which to complete the project. My mother, no more comfortable at a sewing machine than I was, offered as much help as she could.

But after hours of sewing and resewing, the interfacing didn't lie flat, the sleeves pulled in awkward, ill-fitting directions, the darts puckered at the tip, and the fabric, no matter how many times we laundered it, remained scratchy, stiff, and rumpled.

JUNE 11:

Was that fashion show a farce! I felt so awkward, like such an ass!

P.S. People are so cruel!

What prompted the postscript I can't remember. Did I get heckled? Did Mrs. Cooke criticize the way I walked? We'd spent hours reviewing the proper way to move our feet, to walk as models do. "Take your time," Mrs. Cooke told us. "Look ahead of you, into the distance, not at your feet or the audience, and think of something slightly amusing that you have to keep secret. Don't hurry. This is your moment to shine."

Not my moment. My dress itched me and was cut too tight under the arms. It was blazingly hot on the shadeless patio. Our mothers sat together on folding chairs, fanning themselves with the mimeographed programs. "You couldn't ask for a better day for a fashion show," said Mrs. Eisen, who'd stopped by along with some of the other women teachers. No one mentioned the boys gawking at us through the windows facing the patio, making faces or holding their stomachs while they cracked up. They weren't asked to parade around displaying the metal or wood projects they worked on in shop—and even if they had, it wouldn't have been the equivalent of what we had been called on to do. Our persons were being scrutinized, our actual physical selves: the way we walked, paused, stood, held our arms and necks, positioned our feet.

When my turn came to walk the runway, I very nearly froze. "Go!" Anna said, propelling me into the sole spotlight, the deserted concrete walkway. What happened next, as I walked into that humming, damp throng of gathered women, is that they subsumed me, overpowered me, and I disappeared, vaporized into the June sun, turned into an ambulatory dress and jacket. It's possible to lose track of yourself, to become just a head, a mind, some kind of disembodied consciousness. Neither boy nor girl, nothing, just an entity taking a long walk on an excruciatingly hot day, I walked, pirouetted, stood, and walked back.

During that walk, I realize now, I buried Rutherford. But from every death springs a new life, and what emerged was Roberta, alone for the first time in her life—without much of a sense of what to do next.

In the end, Mrs. Cooke had the last laugh. Over the ensuing years, as I retreated into domesticity—my bedroom, the library, the dorm, various apartments—I lost sight of myself, in an almost literal way. Selecting a college was torture: I tried two and felt at home at neither. I never questioned that I'd major in English and go on to study comparative literature or the nineteenth-century novel, but when it came time to apply for graduate school, I couldn't bring myself to begin the process. While my colleagues ran around procuring recommendations and transcripts for their applications, I discovered that I liked to bake, to make pies and cakes, eventually bread; that I enjoyed quilting, embroidery, cross-stitching, even sewing. Though I kept in only sporadic touch with them, I knew that Beth and Denise were also in a kind of limbo. The fall Alice took her first graduate psychology course, I took a job as a secretary to a research radiologist.

I wanted to get married and have children—goals I couldn't articulate to myself or others, given the feminist times, but that thoroughly defined my movement through my twenties and thirties. "Teaching is a good job for a woman," my family had always told me, advice that made me roll my eyes but that I nonetheless followed. I taught, married, conceived, wrote, and cultivated a very private persona.

I didn't become a homemaker, but the life I've pieced together resembles my mother's more closely than it does either my sister's or any of my close friends'. Much to my surprise, I discovered after my first son was born that I simply couldn't leave him for big chunks of time. Writing and teaching were activities I could fit in depending on his schedule and the availability of baby-sitters. This patchwork allowed me to work in ways that were meaningful, and at the same time be home to make dinner most nights, take clothing to the dry cleaners, pick up my children from school.

Since I work at home, I'm constantly reminding my sons that I do indeed work, but they rarely see me at it, since my work time is defined by their absence. To the women with whom I greet the school bus I am just like them, a suburban housewife who spends her time running to the supermarket and on errands. I have dinner on the table each night at six o'clock.

I don't have a schedule of doing wash, and I never get around to vacuuming my sofas; in many ways my household is much more scattershot than my mom's or Mrs. Cooke's. But the thought of working full time and all it entails—in terms of both time away from my home and family, and the kind of visibility and Rutherford-like competition into which I'd have to enter—daunts me.

Only within the past two years have I become aware of the fact that I want a more public life, a life beyond the kitchen and the bus stop, even beyond my study, where I sit in relative isolation with my thoughts. With encouragement, I've joined several community and religious organizations, but the voice to use at these meetings and committees is so rusty that I spend most of my time throat-clearing.

Just last year I had as embarrassing a moment as any I'd endured in Mrs. Cooke's fashion show. During an impassioned debate at a synagogue board meeting, I found myself in a claustrophobically small minority, siding with just one other woman, whom I knew only slightly but admired enormously, against a vocal, outraged majority. Despite her eloquent arguments, the motion we supported failed miserably. I could hardly wait until the meeting was adjourned so I could tell her how much I'd agreed with what she'd said. "Then why didn't you say so?" she thundered. I flushed, stammered, gasped; of all the responses I expected her to have, this one hadn't crossed my mind. I wanted simply to flee, but she wouldn't let me. If gazes had hooks, she reeled me in.

I had no answer—or rather, I had a thousand answers, a million excuses, all of which surfaced during the ride home. I was too timid to speak up in front of a hostile group; I couldn't keep track of my thoughts; she was so eloquent that anything I thought to add would be redundant; perhaps issues were involved of which I knew nothing; the people at the meeting were virtual strangers and I wanted them to think well of me, as if I were a dress to be tried on and found "becoming"; I didn't want to be disagreed with or thought foolish. Mostly, though, I was afraid of my own feelings, of my own vehemence—of my disdain for those arguing against me. These snowballing fears had silenced me, much to my great shame. That night in my car, as I drove home from the meeting, my cheeks red, my pulse racing, Rutherford's eyelids fluttered for the first time in thirty years.

And he continues to stir, at the oddest times. Buying clothes, putting together outfits from the odds and ends in my closet, applying makeup, I find myself thinking back to art, to Miss Castro's pots of paint and drawers of many-textured materials. Listening to Billie Holiday CDs in the car, I remember that the thing I first wanted to be—before hairdresser, long before archaeologist—was a singer, not one who sang in a chorus, blending her voice into others, but a soloist, front and center stage, in a bright-red dress, caressing a microphone, singing her heart out. Watching the Mark Morris dance company, I remember our modern-dance unit in gym and think how it would feel to own my body as dancers do, to possess it, to thrust it forward and toss it however I please.

Both Rutherford and Roberta spurned these electives in eighth grade; relegated to the trash heap, these periods were wastes of time, colossal bores, subjects neither boys nor girls were interested in.

But now the immediacy of art, dance, and music, the pleasure in the body they bring, the direct appeal to the senses short-circuiting the intellect, all call me. Every day that I sit at my desk moving words around, I wish I could express myself in a more immediate, more spontaneous way. Letter writing is the closest I come to improvisation, to the jazz I now feel thirsty for.

And when I think about going back to school, about all the lessons I'd take if I had nothing to do but study, it's not medical or law school I contemplate, or even comparative lit; I wish I could learn to paint, to dance, to move, to sing, with the same pleasure and authority I remember experiencing for only a short time in my life—when Rutherford was loose on the baseball diamond.

MAY 26:

The play [the twentieth-anniversary production of Tennessee Williams's The Glass Menagerie, *starring Maureen*

> *Stapleton, George Grizzard, Pat Hingle, and Piper Laurie] was unbelievable. The acting was superb. Really, I am kinda disturbed, like after I read* A Separate Peace. *It was absolutely fantastic. . . . The play, oh, the play was too great for words of any kind. I'll never forget it. And Dad wants me to be like the horses, conformed, while I want to be like the unicorn, and stand up and fight. I can't go through life thinking only of myself any more, there's something, I don't know what yet, that is more important than me. I've got to find it! Soon, for it is the essence of life.*

If I close my eyes, I can still recall the delicious sensation of sitting in the darkened theater, surrounded by my English class, not knowing who was where, beyond caring who sat next to whom. The entire dreamscape of a play unfolded over the course of a single heartbeat. I breathed in when it began and out when it was over, afraid, in the interim, to stir, afraid of upsetting one of the glass animals, of breaking the spell under which the actors worked.

I too was under a spell. Williams didn't so much write a play as bring a lantern to a place within the human soul that I'd never glimpsed. That he could evoke so much contradictory feeling at once—ridicule and pity for the mother, pity and frustration for the daughter—and that he could depict both men with equal measures of exasperation and acceptance, exercised my heart as nothing else ever had.

I suppose I identified with the cripple, unmarriageable

as she was, even as I knew that I stood a better chance than she did of ever escaping from home. But mostly I loved being alone with the play, and with the experience—which had never before visited me during the musicals I'd been to, or even during the performance of *The Birds*—of having the playwright gently flay my skin and expose my quivering nerves, allowing his characters and their ineffable feelings to pluck at me as I sat in a public place in the midst of my classmates, most of whom were uncharacteristically and similarly stunned into a private, appreciative silence.

A brisk three days later, I took another trip, in an entirely different direction—to the Flushing World's Fair, to perform a few brief songs with the chorus. The only part of the concert I recall today—besides the scorching heat and the fact that we couldn't hear the piano at all and were perpetually, horribly off-key—was a song we didn't sing.

A while back we'd rehearsed a gospel tune, "Rock-a-My Soul in the Bosom of Abraham," which required that we repeat the word "bosom" three times in the first verse. During the initial read-through, we had all cracked up. Then we tried it again, and the tenors and basses broke down again.

After several more tries over the course of the next few rehearsals, there were still a few boys who couldn't pull themselves together. I remember them, basses mostly, sitting in the back row, shading their eyes with their hands, stamping their feet, saying under their breath to Mr. Hammer, "I just can't do it," as if they were being asked to ride a bicycle though they had only one leg.

How childish, we thought, altos and sopranos, *tsk*ing our tongues and rolling our eyes, our indignation uniting us into one collective woman. We'd been forbearing, but now our patience and our good humor had all been exhausted. Mr. Hammer exhaled slowly, sharing his exasperation with the two sections of girls flanking the boys, shrugging his shoulders slightly as if to say, "Can you believe how ridiculous they are?" He put down his baton, put one hand on his hip, and with the other raked his curly blond hair. "You're ridiculous," he said, staring at the boys struggling for self-control. "Impossible. Pull yourselves together."

But they couldn't. We gave the song another try. Then, without a word, Mr. Hammer folded the music, jammed it in his folder, and glared at the offenders for a full five minutes.

"'Michael Row Your Boat Ashore,'" he said quietly to Ilene, his way of introducing a song. He spoke to her confidentially, as if she were his peer and not one of our classmates. He picked up his baton and was about to begin. But then he paused and walked over to the piano. "Unbelievable," he said under his breath to Ilene. Shaking her head, she smiled uneasily. What else could she have done? Something wasn't right. Sure, the boys had been reprimanded, humiliated. They'd failed an important test. But on the other hand, we'd abandoned the song. They'd prevailed, those snickering boys, snickering still. And though Mr. Hammer's every gesture aligned him with us, we could see, Ilene up close and my fellow sopranos in the last row, that something in him was quietly, unquenchably chuckling.

Our dismal World's Fair performance behind us, we were free to go off on our own for a few hours. Mr. Hammer, Ilene, and several other kids from the chorus banded together and decided to get something to eat. People quickly paired off, and I found myself left more or less alone. Mrs. Hammer approached me, asked if I wanted to walk around with her for a while. I was grateful for the company. We agreed to first get something to drink and then take in some of the attractions.

The day was hot and blindingly sunny. I remember standing on line for a Coke, shading my eyes with my hand, and trying to decide how to spend the afternoon. Countless diversions surrounded us, all of them noisy, hot, with long lines and relentless sun.

"Well," said Mrs. Hammer, terminally perky. She must have been a cheerleader, I thought, and not so many years ago. "Where do we start?" She was eager; there was a bounce in her step.

What was wrong with me? Didn't I know how to have fun? This was the World's Fair, for goodness' sake, a thousand delights at my fingertips. I closed my eyes and remembered the cloistered darkness of the Brooks Atkinson Theater, where a crippled girl tended to her glass menagerie. The memory belonged to another country. I held dual citizenship, there and here, and though each negated the other, I couldn't entirely give either up.

JUNE 1:

Started studying cit. ed. for final. Another A+ *on reaction paper. It's late.*

After May's flurry of activities and border crossings, June ushered in the folding of the academic tents. As summer approached, school took on the inconstant, slightly shabby appearance of any other time-bound diversion—a beach house left empty for the winter months, or a traveling carnival that had to be set up each year and then packed away—the concept of school enduring more than any particular class, teacher, or subject. School in June whispers of limitless time, of transience, of vacant space. Time to review the year, to look back on old notes, to underline essential facts, to shake the beach blanket of the year and see what flies away, what settles back down. Time to circulate autograph books among friends and accost teachers after school or in the halls, asking them to write a few words.

To Roberta, All the best wishes in the world. Such a pleasure to have had you in class! Ruth Villard, Math 8, 1964–65.

The annual Honor Society induction dinner was held at a local restaurant. Of our circle of friends, only Rod and I were inducted. Various members of the faculty, including Mr. Black, joined us at the restaurant. Also attending were the student teacher who had worked with Mr. Black during the past few months and her supervisor from the local college, who, after hearing my name, informed me that though I'd given his student quite a challenge, she'd emerged a better teacher, in large part thanks to me.

"I felt immensely proud," I wrote that night. "I hope everyone is immensely jealous of me. I worked damn hard and I loved like hell being there."

When it was time to be called to the podium to receive our individual handshake, scroll, and commemorative pin, who should be doling out the goods but Mrs. Cooper, her hair teased to new heights and new pointiness—a virtual crown of dyed blue-black thorns—resplendent in orange chiffon and spike heels to match. "Well," she said, studying me as she handed me my award, "you finally made it after all."

"I smiled," I wrote later in my diary, "but I wanted to sock her."

I was cranky. The prospect of the summer always daunted me, an endless lunch period, or weekend, time away from school, from my friends, from work, all of which gave me structure and meaning. What would I do with myself?

And I hated saying good-bye—to everyone, it seemed, except, perhaps, Mrs. Cooper.

> To Roberta: You certainly have been one of the finest students it has been my pleasure to teach. You have that fine quality, much maturity, and are among the finest young ladies it has been my pleasure to know. Much luck and success. Philip Black.

The approaching end of year affected everyone. Mr. Black threw an uncharacteristic tantrum in class one day while preparing us for our final. After asking a question to which no one knew the answer, he grew red in the face and told us to stop taking notes, to simply sit and listen—and remember. "As of this moment," he promised, "I'm rewriting your final. It's all ready, in my desk at home, but I'm going to make up a new one. A harder one. The hardest one I've ever prepared."

Later he apologized and took back all his threats, but I was still furious at him. "He wants me to get a 100, or at least a 95 on the final. I swear, it's too demanding. I hate when someone else sets my standards for me!"

> Chere Roberte, J'espere que vous aurez toujours la bonne chance!!! A. Rizzoli.

Finals were over on June 23. "92 on cit. ed. test!" I wrote that night. "Everyone was quiet, waiting, and then pow, he announced it, 92—the highest grade in every class. I was so thrilled! 'You've got it made,' Mr. Black told me"—a comment no different than hundreds of others he'd showered upon me all year. This time, however, his words were an annoyance, something to swat away, background static obscuring the real message. I'd mastered his curriculum; he'd taught me to think critically, an invaluable skill, for which I'm indebted to him. But when I examined our relationship, I realized the degree to which he'd isolated me, become leery of me, the way he propelled me forward and drew me back. The term was finally over; I'd had enough of him and anything he could say.

To Roberta:

Six things there are that spell content,
Six things that mean a life well spent:
A peaceful mind, a grateful heart,
A love for all that's true,
A helping hand, real tolerance,
And lots of things to do.

Jane Johnson, English 8 Honors.

LAST DAY

June 25. We had only one period—homeroom—during which we received our report cards. In the sixth and final marking period, I'd finally achieved the goal toward which I'd been working all year: first honors, all *A*'s—"shock of shocks," I wrote later that night.

We were dismissed by ten o'clock. What I'd been trained to do, to do well in school, suddenly wasn't my job anymore. As if I'd gotten a pink slip, I found myself unemployed.

To celebrate our first day of vacation, Beth, Alice, and I decided to ride our bikes to Cold Spring Harbor, a picturesque village a few miles to the northeast, on Long Island Sound.

We pedaled through town, a cluster of old stores near the railroad station, to Northern Boulevard. Quite unexpectedly, the road began a gradual but definite descent, and we found ourselves sailing effortlessly downhill, gaining speed each second. I can still recall the breathless exhilaration I felt—sun on our faces, wind billowing our T-shirts and imploding our attempts at conversation. I was in the lead.

In a park overlooking the harbor, we ate the sandwiches we'd brought from home. My mood that morning had been bittersweet, but no longer. Drunk on our independence, we parked our bikes and walked down the main street, browsing in the quaint bookstore, a bakery, and the whaling museum. None of us wore watches; it was a timeless afternoon.

When we noticed the shadows lengthening, we reluctantly climbed back on our bikes and began the slow ride out of town, promising each other that we'd come back next week. Just a few blocks away, near the fish hatchery, the road began to rise. We tucked our heads down and stood up to try to put more weight behind each pedal, but gravity proved too oppressive. First Beth dismounted, walking her bike up the hill, then Alice. I was the last to give up. I kept thinking that I could force my exhausted legs to keep going, to pedal just a little more until I reached the tavern at the crest of the hill. But eventually I too had to get off my bike and walk it.

We gathered in the parking lot of the tavern. Beth and Alice seemed dusty, tired, and thoroughly dispirited; I, however, was fighting a rising tide of panic: what if we couldn't make it home? This wasn't the end of the hill, just a stopping point. What if we never got home? We didn't even have money to make a phone call, having spent all our change on postcards in the bookstore.

We sat together, gasping for breath like overworked beasts of burden, none of us speaking, all of us reprimanding ourselves for having so little foresight—for having no money, no hats, no drinks, nothing to wipe our sweaty brows with; for failing to realize that after coasting down a hill you had to ride up it.

Eventually we roused ourselves. Past caring how we looked, we stumbled into the bar for a few moments of air-conditioned reprieve, endured the stares of the guffawing patrons, and shamelessly asked for drinks of water. Outside, we wordlessly mounted our bikes and slowly pedaled home. At the corner of Jericho Turnpike we said good-bye to Alice; a few blocks later, Beth turned off for her house, and then I was alone.

I'd always fantasized, riding my bike, that I was teaching a class, instructing those students accompanying me how to be safe and how to enjoy the pleasures of the open road. I'd talk aloud—who could hear me?

But now, riding home, I was silent. Summer vacation, just a few hours old, already felt like an eternity. My panic had dissipated, but so had the morning's exhilaration. That I'd done so well in school was a distant memory, something to report to my grandparents when they called later that evening, my report card a document to place on my father's dresser so he could see it the moment he came home. It was already old, ancient history.

In the present was a gauzy confusion. My sense of not knowing what had once been clear had been building for the past few months, the way someone losing her vision wakes up each morning and finds the world slightly grainier and a shade darker than the day before.

I kept replaying the picture of us in the parking lot of

the tavern. How had we managed to pull off such a fiasco? I'd felt as helpless as—a girl. As a flighty, scatter-brained, helpless girl. A girl who didn't even know when she was asked out on a date. A girl who only liked boys who didn't like her. A girl who couldn't even get herself home.

Yet my confusion was more aural than visual. The voice I was used to hearing—my actual voice, the voice that had always narrated my fantasy, the voice that kept me focused, on track, that spurred me on—was silenced. Or, rather, drowned out by a host of other voices, a commingling of exhortations, pleas, and recriminations, coming from all directions at once. I couldn't hear myself; there was so much I had to listen for.

Of course I did eventually get home. I took a shower, went out to dinner with my family to celebrate the end of school, called my grandparents to tell them my grades, and recovered my equilibrium sufficiently by bedtime to write in my diary, "I love you, and Mr. Black and Whitey and Mrs. Johnson."

Then I signed my name, "Roberta."

On every other page I'd used a nickname—Sues, or Issi. But that night I turned solemn, I suppose in recognition of the passing of the old order, the sense that there was no going back, that the journey home isn't always shorter or easier, that it can take years, sometimes thirty.

EPILOGUE

Last fall I had lunch with Mr. Loehman. In the thirty years since I subscribed to the *Daily Worker* at his suggestion, he's had about six different careers, taught himself three languages, written several books, traveled to the Arctic and the equator; he is at this moment advising government officials of the fledgling republic of Kazakhstan how to move their country into the twentieth century in an economically and environmentally responsible way. We've been in regular touch, mostly through letters, since the year he left my junior high school, but I have also visited him at his home on several occasions, and we've met in various cities for conferences, after which we've taken long walks scouting flea markets and used-book stores.

The last time I saw him, he was staying on Manhattan's Upper West Side, in the apartment of friends who were off on a safari, or an Arctic expedition—all his friends are quietly accomplished in the most exotic ways—and after walking for a bit on Columbus Avenue, we stopped for Chinese-Cuban food. He put on reading glasses to peruse the menu; mine were in my purse. I was nearly twice as old as he had been when he taught me English.

He told me a little about his recently published book, in which he maintains that the environmental challenge has been met, not shirked. Question everything, he had instructed me, have the courage to say the unpopular thing. He asked about my book—this book—and when I told him what it was about, he put down his fork and gave me a scathing look I well remembered.

"You can't tell me things haven't changed since you were a girl." His tone was outraged, not conciliatory. "It's a different world now."

I agreed that it was. Inherent sexism in the classroom, the importance of engaging girls in math and science classes, the entire issue of self-esteem and middle-school-aged girls, the gender biases of teachers from the earliest grades—all these topics are showing up in the morning headlines. The current First Lady doesn't spend any more time talking about White House drapery than Eleanor Roosevelt did. Mr. Loehman's own daughter, for whom Alice and I crocheted an afghan when she was born during our freshman year of college, was at that moment living in Brazil, pursuing graduate studies in ecology.

But I also know that much remains the same—repeated polls indicate that women return from their nine-to-five jobs to work a full second shift around the house; parents gathered in a playground with busy toddlers remark on the girls sitting quietly in the sandbox and the boys swinging from poles and jumping fences—and that some of the changes, a study indicating that college women are becoming more masculine, for example, aren't taking us the in right direction. Typically, though, I had difficulty explaining this to him. It's still hard for me to think deeply without my fingers on a keyboard.

"Send me a copy," he said, shaking his head. "I'll tell you what I think."

Alice and I still speak to each other as regularly as our families will allow, for as many minutes as we can steal. Our conversation, which began in eighth grade, shows no signs of flagging. With her I'm discovering how to pair honesty and garrulity. A psychologist, she's also my personal emotional trainer. Anna became a psychologist also. Beth teaches foreign language; Denise just received tenure as an English professor; both are writers. Ilene teaches music. No mathematicians, no theoretical scientists. We all have children. Rod and Eddie are attorneys.

Recently, my mother asked me to come by and help her clean out the basement, a task she'd been avoiding since my father's death, nearly eight years earlier. Driving through her neighborhood one morning, I took a sudden detour and turned onto the road leading to my old junior high school.

It was late spring. The athletic fields were empty, though a gym class emerged from the building and began picking its lethargic way to the tennis courts, a lazy gaggle of girls wearing shorts and T-shirts, not gym suits. The trees in the distance had grown so tall that the Long Island Expressway was obscured, the sound of traffic muted.

"All Visitors Must Report to Main Office," instructed several signs hung on the front door of the school. Instead, I ambled down the hall, looking at the scrolls listing each of the graduating classes. For a moment I forgot which year I had graduated. There was my name, asterisk-less; I hadn't been a member of the student council in ninth grade, and the fact that I'd served as chair of the election committee wasn't noted.

Farther down the main hallway were the plaques listing each class's elected officers, which had once meant so much to me. They were hung, Ozymandias style, crookedly and randomly, in a dark corner near an exit no one used.

After a few minutes I just started walking—toward the gym and the chorus room, past the three academic wings, surprised to see that the guidance suite, where I'd conferred with Mrs. Eisen, had been changed to a media center. Circling back, I passed the cafeteria—tiny, empty, and more cheerless than I remembered, filled with the chatter of women readying trays of food and silverware.

The building, a perfectly preserved specimen from the sixties, felt terribly out of synch with the up-to-date students straggling in the hallway, kids my son's age, wearing the same baggy jeans, oversized T-shirts, suede sneakers. To them—to everyone, apparently—I was invisible.

In front of the auditorium, I paused, then slipped in through an open door. The room looked timeworn but surprisingly expansive—the seats comfortable and generously spaced, the stage wide and majestic. Risers, probably used by the chorus during its recent spring concert, were still standing. I sat where I had when Mr. Black joined me after I'd lost the election.

Any minute I expected him to saunter in, his grade book on top of a pile of reaction papers he'd just collected and couldn't wait to savage. He'd recognize me in a flash, I knew; he'd shake my hand and kiss me on the cheek. He'd ask me what I was doing with myself.

I'd trot out my impressive-sounding résumé—the Ivy League college and esteemed graduate school I'd attended, the books I'd written, my freelance magazine work. I'd show him pictures of my sons, tell him my husband is a psychologist, that we live only twenty minutes to the east.

But I'd be thinking of my anti-résumé, all the things I didn't do. I never went to medical school, though I thought of it many times; I never became an anthropologist or a warrior against cancer. I never matriculated for a Ph.D. I never ran for office or sought the spotlight, I never tried for a tenure-track job or a job for which promotion was at stake.

"Why didn't you ever once suggest, even intimate, that I should think about becoming a lawyer? Or a doctor? Or any of the professions you must have suggested to Rod and Eddie?" My voice quivers with anger.

I'm using the very voice I lost in these halls, my public voice, Rutherford's voice. I learned to be a girl—to ameliorate and compromise, to accede and self-abnegate—not because I came to value relationships over achievement, not because I didn't want to hurt other people, but because I began to notice that the depth of my own desires—for power, knowledge, recognition—scared Mr. Black, my father, the people around me. And within a short time I was scared of those feelings as well. Better to withdraw, to become private, to trot out my ambition and competition in the solitude of my study, to slather them with words, which I could rework until the hard edge was smoothed, than to speak of them aloud, or act on them.

In a moment my anger's spent. It's not Mr. Black's fault, or my father's. I could have changed course at any moment. Honestly, I'm happiest at my desk, working with words, sifting through my feelings, keeping track of what my friends and I say to each other, what we read, trying to make sense of our lives.

Well, Mr. Black would say, I have to be getting back. Great to see you. And he'd trundle off, looking for someone to tell of our meeting.

He'd be in his sixties by now.

Parked in my mother's driveway was a huge dumpster, brought by the man she hired to fix her roof. As I got out of the car, I saw my mother walk toward it, carrying a lamp fixture I remembered from our Bayside apartment. She heaved it up and over into the mountain of roofing tiles, broken glass, splintered wood. She was near tears.

Like a Red Cross volunteer, I swung into cheerful but determined action, leading her through the kitchen toward the basement and down the wooden steps my father had worn away over the years. In the far corner were clustered the cartons housing my old school papers, in which I'd stumbled on the diaries over a year earlier. Not yet ready to sift through all that, I retreated to the clutter surrounding the upright piano that had mystified my sister and me from the day we spotted it: How had it gotten down here? Had the house been built around it, like a ship in a bottle?

We settled into a routine: I dredged up objects from the various dusty piles and held them out for her inspection: "What about this?" I'd ask. "Save or toss?" She hesitated. "Save or toss?" I asked again, feeling ruthless. She shrugged. "That means toss," I said.

She took to shaking her head in an almost imperceptible way, as if she had a mild form of Parkinson's. In a short time, the area around the stairs was piled high with objects heading for the dumpster.

God, my father had been an industrious man. He'd put aside projects the way prairie housewives did fruit and vegetables for canning: illustrations to be framed, scraps of wood to be turned into vases and pencil holders, greeting cards to assemble into collages, jewelry and handbags needing fixing or restoring. Even if he'd lived to be a hundred and twenty, he'd never have finished everything on his drawing board.

Suddenly I remembered what I'd been looking for that morning when I found my diaries—a piece of cross-stitching my father had promised to frame for me. I'd bought the needlework in a Copenhagen stitchery, at which I felt completely at home despite the language barrier: the clerks, bosomy women who wore their eyeglasses on chains around their necks and their dyed hair up in frowsy buns, reminded me of those in Lower East Side yarn stores to which my grandmother had taken me.

My grandmother taught me to embroider when I was a girl. I remember sitting so close to her I could hear her breath and the flow of her saliva. She put everything in her mouth: the needle while she readied the thread, the tip of the thread—"the cotton," she called it—before knotting it. My first project was a pillowcase. Dutifully I covered each of the faint blue lines with colored thread, practicing the chain stitch, the backstitch, and my favorite, the French knot.

The samplers I bought in Denmark were different. "It's called counted cross-stitch," I told my father, the only one in my family who seemed interested.

"How do you know where to start?" he asked, turning the fabric over in his hand as if it were a book whose pages were glued together.

"You find the center square by folding the fabric in half twice, and then just follow this graph, counting as you go along, in any direction you want." For some reason, we both found this concept fascinating.

As my mother and I lugged stuff out to the dumpster, I asked her if she knew what had happened to my sampler. She suggested we look in the far corner of the basement, an area we'd both assiduously avoided all morning. Power tools—lathes, presses, band saws, one more menacing than the next—marked the outer perimeter of my father's work space, all made from the same battleship gray or green metal, oozing oil and sawdust. We paused at the entrance, hesitant to take another step. A squat section of the front-yard cherry tree he'd cut down stood near the lathe. On a hook were his apron, heavy gloves, and headgear—helmet and goggles—which made him look like a worker sent in to mop up radioactivity after a nuclear accident.

"I think I'll ask Donald"—the man fixing her roof—"if he wants any of this stuff. Your father bought himself very high-quality equipment."

To the right of the lathe stood the bleached skeleton of a cabinet he'd been fashioning for the master bathroom. Inert, abandoned, it looked like a magician's chest. A crouching man could fit inside; I peeked, as if my father could be hiding within, smiling his curious half-smile. I ran my hand over the wood, sanded to such an unnatural smoothness that it felt almost liquefied. He was always proudest of those aspects of his handiwork that weren't immediately apparent—a drawer or a picture frame put together without a single nail.

Incorrigibly neat, he had lined the metal bookshelves with row after row of loose-leaf notebooks holding his woodworking plans; old cigar boxes from the days when he allowed himself a cigar after Sunday lunch, coffee cans—Chock Full o'Nuts from my childhood and, more recently, decaffeinated brands—holding screws, bolts, washers, each meticulously labeled; baby-food jars—from which, once, my sister, now thirty-five years old, was fed—containing clear solvents. I opened one, releasing pungent fumes, which snaked right up my nose and stung me like ammonia.

Screwdrivers, drills, wrenches, pliers, hammers, awls, levels, and sanders in every conceivable size, their wooden handles stained with his sweat, hung on a huge pegboard. Here was the little stool he'd made for me, which I helped paint blue, his first big project when we still lived in an apartment in Queens. A cast-off alarm clock, which used to sit next to his bed. Discarded key rings. On our old kitchen table from Queens stood a rough-cut toy elephant, with four chunky feet, a trunk, and eight holes in its back—a crayon holder for my son. Propped up against a bottle of Elmer's glue were the plans and a can of blue paint. He'd sanded it—the wood satiny smooth, the fragment of sandpaper right there. In a pile of sawdust I saw my father's fingerprints.

Like counted cross-stitch, this shantytown, this Hooverville, assembled from the detritus of our family life, had begun as an inner sanctum, gradually sprawled outward toward ungainly suburbs. My father—brimming over with feelings he couldn't name or give vent to except fitfully, with great embarrassment—had created an underground retreat even more private than his bedroom, directly above it, more personal than an undergarment.

"I have to go upstairs," my mother said. "I've had enough for today."

I remained in my father's workroom, trespassing everywhere, opening each box and jar and notebook. I found a complete set of Matchbox cars; why hadn't he given them to my son? I found a pencil holder I'd made in fourth grade. I found a pair of pearlized eyeglasses my grandmother wore when we watched *The Ed Sullivan Show* and embroidered together.

This was Rutherford's room, containing my father's legacy to me. He'd probably hoped that I would take his tools, incorporate them into my life, use them. And I had, though not in the way he intended. Here in the basement, face-to-face with the boy my father wished I would become, I said a final, tearful good-bye to both of them. Over the past few years I'd begun to emerge from the crucible of eighth grade: the novel I'd begun, the tennis lessons I'd signed up for, the committees I'd agreed to serve on, defined a new yet familiar direction. Using my diary as a guidebook, I had set about reclaiming the public life I'd sacrificed, the full-blooded voice I'd muted, the powerful swing I'd interrupted thirty years before. Rutherford's voice was now inseparably entwined with Roberta's; finally, I felt as if no part of me was expendable.

My mother called to me from the kitchen door. "Did you find what you were looking for? The sampler?"

Yes and no, I thought. It will turn up one day—most everything does. What's lost rarely remains so. Even when you're sure something is gone for good, it's probably just changed into something else. As my father would say, if he were suddenly to materialize, as I still sometimes expect him to, the mark of a good seamstress is not on the front of her handiwork but on the back. The trick is knowing where to look.